T0340390

MAKING RISKY
AND **IMPORTANT**
DECISIONS
A Leader's Guide

MAKING RISKY AND IMPORTANT DECISIONS
A Leader's Guide

Ruth Murray-Webster
David Hillson

CRC Press
Taylor & Francis Group
Boca Raton London New York

CRC Press is an imprint of the
Taylor & Francis Group, an **informa** business

AN AUERBACH BOOK

Dedication

Take good counsel and accept correction—that's the way to live wisely and well.

— Proverbs 19:20 from *The Message*[*]

---

[*] Peterson, E. H. (2002). *The Message: The Bible in Contemporary Language*. NavPress.

Contents

List of Figures
and Tables

Foreword

As a senior leader in a global company, it's clear that making risky decisions is a critical part of leadership and that it's important to build an organization that can make those decisions in a consistent way, aligned with corporate objectives.

This was always difficult, but in a world that is changing quickly, society demands much of leaders as they balance seemingly incompatible objectives and related risks. As the bar is raised, so leaders everywhere need to continually improve.

I really like this book—it covers a lot in a relatively small number of words and is clearly written, providing practical and pragmatic guidance on making difficult decisions in the real world.

— Mark Davies
Group Executive Safety, Technical & Projects
Rio Tinto plc

Foreword

Preface

When we first met in the late 1990s, our approach to life and business was very different. You might characterize one as "hard" and the other as "soft," focusing on either process or people. But as we developed mutual regard and respect for one another, we began a productive collaboration that changed each of us. After over two decades of working together, we're convinced that you don't have to choose between process and people: both are vital.

Both of us are fascinated by ideas, but only insofar as they are practical in addressing real-world issues. Our early work together developed and applied novel approaches for consultancy clients, helping them resolve tough challenges in their projects and businesses. Recognizing that our ideas would be useful to more than just our own clients, we started to write books together, sharing our insights for others to pick up and use.

Our early books tackled two big topics: risk attitude and risk appetite. Drawing on academic thinking and practical experience, together with our own focused research, we explained how to understand and manage risk attitude, for both individuals and groups. We developed a robust language for describing risk appetite and showed how to express and use risk appetite in practice.

Despite our best intentions to introduce these new concepts in a way that was easy to apply, we've often felt that we could do better. We know our ideas work in practice, because we use them regularly in our own work and when we're supporting others. Previously we've explained the "what" and only touched on the "how." In this book the "how" takes center stage. We have taken all the ideas from our previous books (and some new ones), added our wide and varied experience in putting them into practice, and applied them to a specific challenge that's faced by all leaders: *How to make risky and important decisions.* Making these types of decisions is difficult but necessary. Our hope is that you find practical and effective help through this collection of the fruits of our long friendship and collaboration.

— Ruth Murray-Webster and David Hillson
October 2020

About the Authors

Dr. Ruth Murray-Webster is recognized as a leader of project-based organizational change and risk management, performing roles as a practitioner, advisor, facilitator, researcher, and author. For more than 30 years, Ruth has practiced and advanced change and risk management approaches, developing commercially astute strategy centered around emerging risks and disruptive trends.

Ruth has experience in delivering change objectives in most sectors.

Prior to returning to her own company, Potentiality UK, in 2018, Ruth held appointments as Director, Change Portfolio and Group Head of Risk for a major port operator and Director, Risk in the Boardroom practice for KPMG LLP. Ruth researched organizational change from the perspective of the recipients of change for an Executive Doctorate at Cranfield School of Management between 2008 and 2012. She is an Associate Fellow at the University of Oxford Saïd Business School, where she supports senior leaders on the Major Projects Leadership Academies for the UK and Australian governments and as Head Tutor for the University of Oxford Leading Strategic Projects online program.

Ruth's interest in risk management arose from a passion to help organizations to take educated risks, not avoid them. She has co-authored numerous books on the human aspects of risk management and has published papers in the areas of project complexity, organizational ambidexterity through projects and programs, and multi-paradigmatic perspectives on business transformation programs. Ruth was Lead Editor of the Association for Project Management *Body of Knowledge,* 7th edition (2019) and the 5th edition of *Managing Successful Programmes*™ (2020). She is currently working on the 6th edition of the Chartered Institute of Building *Code of Practice for Project Management in the Built Environment.*

Ruth was awarded an Honorary Fellowship of the Association for Project Management (APM) in 2013 for her services to risk and change. The synergies between the two disciplines continue to drive Ruth's thinking, writing, and practice.

Known globally as *The Risk Doctor*, **Dr. David Hillson** is recognized as a ground-breaking thinker and expert practitioner in risk management, and he has made several innovative contributions to the discipline, which have been widely adopted.

David has a reputation as an excellent speaker and presenter on risk. His talks blend thought leadership with practical application, presented in an accessible style that combines clarity with humor, guided by the Risk Doctor motto: *"Understand profoundly so you can explain simply."*

He also writes widely on risk, with twelve major books and over 100 professional papers. He publishes a regular Risk Doctor Briefing blog in seven languages to 10,000 followers and has over 10,000 subscribers to the RiskDoctorVideo YouTube channel (www.youtube.com/RiskDoctorVideo).

David has advised leaders and organizations in nearly 60 countries around the world on how to create value from risk based on a mature approach to risk management, and his wisdom and insights are in high demand. He has also advised on strategic risk at the national leadership level for several nations facing radical change.

David Hillson's ground-breaking work in risk management for over three decades has been recognized with a wide range of awards. David is a Chartered Fellow of the Institute of Risk Management (IRM), and he was named their inaugural Risk Personality of the Year in 2010-2011, recognizing his significant global contribution to improving risk management and advancing the risk profession. David is also an Honorary Fellow of the UK Association for Project Management (APM) and a PMI Fellow in the Project Management Institute (PMI®), both marking his contribution to developing project risk management.

David was elected a Fellow of the Royal Society of Arts (RSA) to contribute to its Risk Commission, and he led the RSA Fellows project on societal attitudes to failure. He is also a Chartered Fellow of the Chartered Management Institute (CMI).

Chapter 1

Doing Better

As a leader, a large part of your role is to make decisions. Sometimes you will make decisions alone, other times as part of a decision-making group with your senior operations team, as part of project governance, or with your board or trustees. Decisiveness—the ability to make decisions quickly and effectively—is a highly valued trait of leaders in many cultures, and most leaders accept the challenge (and maybe the burden) of taking decisions with and on behalf of their organization.

There are many models and approaches to decision making, but the general consensus is that decision making is about choosing from a number of options or alternatives and doing so as rationally as possible.

The different options you have available for a decision will all have pros and cons in relation to your objectives. Some of those pros and cons will be facts now, others will be uncertain but would have an impact on your objectives if they occurred: risks. Throughout this book, when we use the term *risk,* we are talking about "uncertainties that matter" (Hillson, 2003). Many things are uncertain, but whether those uncertainties occur would not matter to our objectives and the decision in hand. Some uncertainties would matter if they occurred, leading either to a negative impact on objectives and the decision (threats, or *downside* risks) or to a positive impact on objectives and the decision (opportunities, or *upside* risks).

A "good" decision takes into account both what's known (facts) and what's uncertain (risks) at the point of making the decision. As a result, the choice of what to do and what not to do is made with "eyes open," acknowledging the context for making the decision (e.g., how urgent it is or the people who will be impacted) and with a commitment to action from the team. That action may be to do something differently, or to continue as before: without commitment the decision can only be good in theory, not in practice.

You know all this, but you also know that underneath these simple statements is much complexity, that gaining agreement on objectives is not always easy, that identifying and evaluating the range of options and alternatives takes time to do well, and that, even faced with great information about facts and risks, the way forward is not always obvious to everyone.

It's easy to be a great decision maker in hindsight. We are not going to spend time in this book unpicking past decisions and saying what was great or what could have been done differently. Our objective is to help you hone your skills with foresight: to help you navigate your complex world and discharge your responsibilities in the best way you can.

1.1 All Decisions Are Equal, but Some Are More Equal than Others

Borrowing an idea from George Orwell's *Animal Farm* novel (1945), all decisions are equal in that they are important to the people involved at the point of making the decision and committing to action. The decision may be personal, it may be to vary a routine pattern of past decisions, it may be tactical to achieve a short-term goal, or it may be strategic with longer-term implications for many people. The core principles are the same—you need to understand:

- **Objectives:** What is at stake? How will you measure success?
- **Context:** What is the environment or wider system into which this decision fits?
- **Options:** The "change nothing" baseline plus the implications of other alternatives.
- **Commitment to action:** Of yourself and your team.

We say that some decisions are "more equal than others" because they are particularly risky and important. You need to understand the same four points listed above, but doing so is much more complex, and the stakes are higher—for you, your team, your stakeholders.

Decisions are risky and important when:

- The impact on strategic or long-term operational objectives is significant.
- The context is complex, unstable, or changing.
- There is a significant amount of risk associated with different options, and comparing options and their impact on objectives is not straightforward.
- There is no guarantee of commitment from the people who you need to support in order to implement the chosen outcome.

There are many decisions you will make as a leader that do not meet these criteria. Sometimes the impact of the decision on objectives is not very consequential. Often the data on variables (facts or risks) are not extensive and can be easily processed and/or are well understood by a diverse group of decision makers. Although the guidance in this book can be applied to all decisions, in practice only a subset of decisions will be important enough to warrant your close attention.

For those particularly risky and important decisions, those that are "more equal than others," this book will help you to lead the decision-making process with greater knowledge of the pitfalls and greater insight into how you can lead to get the best possible decision in the situation.

1.2 Four Key Questions

In order to get the best possible decision in a risky and important situation, you need to be able to answer the following questions:

- How much risk is too much risk for my organization?
- How is my personal view influencing my judgment?
- How can I balance reason and intuition?
- How can I inspire and embed the behaviors needed to build an effective culture?

1.2.1 How Much Risk Is Too Much Risk for My Organization?

In the past decade, the language of risk appetite and risk capacity has gained a far greater prominence than in previous years. For example, directors and trustees on the boards of listed companies (Financial Reporting Council, 2014) and registered charities (The Charity Commission, 2017) in the UK are required to express the appetite to take risk to pursue shareholder and stakeholder value. Other jurisdictions have similar requirements. Increasingly, value is expressed using the concept of the "triple bottom line": profit, people, and planet (Slaper & Hall, 2011). Risk appetite is therefore not just about how much money you are prepared to chance, but about defining tolerable levels of performance for non-financial objectives in tricky areas such as ethics and sustainability.

If the capacity to bear risk is seen in purely financial terms, it becomes about the strength of the balance sheet and credit ratings with lenders. In a triple-bottom-line world, risk capacity is also about reputation. How much stakeholder trust do you have? What are the bounds of your "licence to operate" with the public?

These are tough questions that you need to be able to answer to make a good decision in a risky and important situation. Many organizations struggle to express risk appetite and risk capacity in a meaningful way. Boards discuss and sign off on statements and build in criteria to risk policies and procedures, but operationalizing these in a meaningful way to support decision making is a difficult task for many executive and senior teams. In Chapter 2 we build up a model that enables you to consider how risk appetite and risk capacity fit alongside other decision variables and where you can make choices about how informed to be at the point of taking the decision.

1.2.2 How Is My Personal View Influencing My Judgment?

There's good news and bad news about the human brain when it comes to risky decision making. We are created and have evolved as a species to be efficient when we need to make routine decisions. Once you've learned how to cross the road safely, you do it without much conscious thought.

When you've decided to trust a particular person, you don't question their objectives and intentions every day. When you've built up a track record of success at work, maybe you start to believe that you are good at this and can handle most situations. Is that rational?

Behavioral economists and risk psychologists have demonstrated time and again that we are far from rational when it comes to making judgments and choices in the face of uncertainty. There is a big literature on this, a few Nobel prizes, and some great readable books. Appendix A provides a list of our favorite further reading, linking the work of other authors into what we say here.

Our own previous work also forms a foundation for this book, as described in Appendix B. For example, in our books on risk attitude (Hillson & Murray-Webster, 2007; Murray-Webster & Hillson, 2008), we addressed the multiple influences on our personal perceptions of risky and important situations.

We elaborate on this in Chapter 3, helping you to consider how judgments become biased so you can then do something about it. For now, consider how your views and judgments are shaped by things such as:

- Past experience
- Past success
- Recency of information
- Who provided the data
- How information was presented/how the story was told
- Your desire for harmony in the team
- Your feelings about people or your personal goals

1.2.3 How Can I Balance Reason and Intuition?

We are a species that "feels" as much as we "think." You have a psychological preference for the degree to which you are drawn to data, facts, rationality—the ability to see, hear, taste, touch, or smell something—compared to the degree to which you are drawn to intuition, disputed/contested "facts," possibilities, and maybe a "sixth sense." No person is either fully rational or completely intuitive. Differences are good and can create value if harnessed. If you only listen to people like you, what are you missing?

To balance reason and intuition, everyone needs to acknowledge what they bring to the situation (positive or negative baggage, future aspirations), appreciate what others bring, assess the situation, and act in a way that helps the decision at hand in its context. That may be to intervene, to assert your own viewpoint and try to change the direction of travel, or to accept things as they are.

This is the most difficult part of decision making for many leaders, particularly if you are working in a culture in which everyone looks to you to be a single decisive voice—or you feel that's what you should be doing. The decisions you make impact you, your employees, customers, investors, regulators, etc. Making good decisions in difficult situations is no small feat, because these types of decisions involve change, uncertainty, anxiety, stress, and sometimes the unfavorable reactions of others. Often leaders are reluctant to overtly acknowledge these difficulties, preferring to just say, "It's the way it is." We believe it's important to acknowledge the challenges and strive to continually improve in this area, because the stakes for organizations are high when sub-optimal decisions are made.

In Chapter 4 we consider what it takes to be competent as an individual decision maker, and we explore the features of a functioning decision-making group. Chapter 5 then provides a process that will help you to improve the outcome of your decision by intentionally addressing hidden influences.

1.2.4 How Can I Inspire and Embed the Behaviors Needed to Build an Effective Culture?

"No man is an Island, entire of itself; every man is a piece of the Continent, a part of the main." (Donne, 1624)

There are many definitions of culture, and applications to organizations (from families to churches to companies) to nations and ethnicities. Culture is part of the context for any decision, because it shapes the expectations and behaviors of others in response to the decision. It is also an influence on the decision-making group itself. You influence the culture as a leader whether or not you intend to or consciously think about it.

Risk culture is a subset of overall organizational culture, and in risky and important situations, it cannot be ignored. We view culture as the environment in which certain behaviors and characteristics are allowed to flourish—or not. Decisions are definitely made in the light of the prevailing culture, and risky and important decisions are specifically influenced by risk culture. You may be trying to change the culture in your area of leadership. The decisions you make are noticeable signals of whether you are endorsing the current behaviors and characteristics or being a role model for what you want in future.

In Chapter 6 we will provide guidance about the interplay between decisions and culture, and we'll discuss what you can do to change that if you need to.

1.3 Why "Doing Better"?

This chapter title suggests that you can improve the way that you take decisions and lead decision making—engaging with your team and considering and communicating what's important about decision making and decisiveness in your organization.

Not everyone will need to take all the medicine! We offer these insights as a way for you to decide where you need to focus in order to make better decisions in risky and important situations.

We don't apologize, however, for our view that everyone can continually improve. The context for our decisions is changing, and in many situations, it's becoming more complex. We all have information from many more sources than we had in the past: it can sound deafening. What do we listen to? What do we ignore? We have both technological advancement and social expectations about the role that technology plays in our lives progressing at a pace like never before. The context for decisions may once have been limited to our company or our industry sector. Today, the growth in global connectedness and the increased awareness and influence of politics and social policy creates a wider and more complex context and introduces risks—threats and opportunities—that we would be foolish to ignore. We fail to understand the underlying systems associated with our work at our peril. We are experiencing disruption that feels unprecedented in our lifetimes: How do we make decisions informed with as much foresight as possible? How do we respond in a way that creates as much value as possible?

Our experience is that often decisions are made without considering the available information or without asking the right questions. Decisions are communicated as if they are rational and objective, yet they are often deeply subjective and flawed. No decision is ever perfect; indeed, the decision outcome, what happens, is not a foregone conclusion of a "good" decision at the point of making it.

In the intervening time between making a decision and the outcome from that decision, many other things may have changed that were entirely unforeseeable in advance. Many people invest in stocks but do not realize a profit, but this doesn't necessarily mean that the original investment decision was poor, based on available information at the time. Sometimes we're just unlucky. Conversely, just because there is a good outcome doesn't mean the original decision was good. You and your children may arrive safely at your destination after driving down the motorway above the speed limit, influenced by alcohol, and with your children unrestrained in the back seat. That's lucky!

It's not rational to judge the quality of a decision in hindsight based on the outcome; the only point of control available is the decision-making process. Despite the lack of total certainty that any decision will lead to the outcomes we desire, we can do better in making decisions that have the best possible chance of achieving our objectives.

In this short book, we summarize our previous work together and our current thinking on risky and important decision making. It is a guide for leaders. We will avoid the underpinning academic arguments, although we acknowledge here that we stand on the shoulders of giants in bringing these ideas to this audience. We focus on providing you with a practical and usable guide, grounded in sound thinking and packaged so you can use it on your own and with your teams.

In the chapters that follow, we focus on the following aspects of making risky and important decisions:

- **Intelligent process:** The variables involved and the choices you can make (Chapter 2)
- **Perception is reality:** Understanding the factors that influence the perception of the people involved and lead to faulty thinking (Chapter 3)
- **Value from difference:** Assembling competent individuals and functional decision-making groups who can intervene to correct faulty thinking, recognizing that value is created from difference, and good decisions rarely come from people who all think in the same way (Chapter 4)

- **Intentional choices:** Finding ways to become aware of what influences your perception of risk, allowing you to choose an appropriate response (Chapter 5)
- **Shaping risk culture:** Demonstrating and building appropriate behaviors for effective decision making (Chapter 6)
- **Yes, but . . . :** Common problems and how to avoid them (Chapter 7)

1.4 Key Points

In this chapter, we've highlighted the following key points:

1. A "good" decision takes account of both facts and uncertainties.
2. Risky and important decisions have significant strategic impact, a complex and changing context, unclear options, and no guaranteed stakeholder commitment.
3. To make a "good" risky and important decision, you need to define risk appetite and risk capacity, understand what influences your judgment, be able to balance reason and intuition, and embed appropriate behaviors in the culture.
4. Making better decisions is both possible and essential!

1.5 Looking Forward

In Chapter 2 we outline the things you need to consider when making a risky and important decision. You have some choices to make of how to go forward, and we'll outline these for you so you can decide how informed you need to be to best serve your organization.

References

Donne, J. (2015). *Devotions upon Emergent Occasions*, edited by J. Sparrow. Cambridge, UK: The University Press. (Original publication date: 1624)

Financial Reporting Council. (2014). *Guidance on Risk Management, Internal Control and Related Financial and Business Reporting*. London, UK: Financial Reporting Council.

Hillson, D. A. (2003). *Effective Opportunity Management for Projects*. Boca Raton, FL: Taylor & Francis, p. 12.

Hillson, D. A., and Murray-Webster, R. (2007). *Understanding and Managing Risk Attitude*, 2nd edition. Aldershot, UK: Gower Publishing.

Murray-Webster, R., and Hillson, D. A. (2008). *Managing Group Risk Attitude*. Aldershot, UK: Gower Publishing.

Orwell, G. (1945). *Animal Farm: A Fairy Story.* London, UK: Secker and Warburg.

Slaper, T. F., and Hall, T. J. (2011). The triple bottom line: What is it and how does it work? *Indiana Business Review*, 86(1).

The Charity Commission. (2017). *Charity Governance Code.* London, UK: The Charity Commission.

Chapter 2

Intelligent Process

As a leader, you constantly make decisions that are both risky and important, but how? In this chapter, we explore what goes into making a risky and important decision, and we build a decision-making model that gives you some choices about the degree to which you want to be informed as a leader.

As outlined in Chapter 1, before you can make a decision, you need to understand:

1. What you need to achieve as a result of this decision (objectives)
2. The situation in which you're making a decision (context)
3. The alternatives that you have to choose between and how each of these would impact the objectives (options)
4. Whether your team will be willing and able to implement the decision (commitment to action)

2.1 Decision Information

The information needed to make a risky and important decision includes the decision objectives to be achieved, the context within which the decision is being made, and the decision options that you're considering.

2.1.1 Objectives

Your organization has *objectives* at various levels—strategic, tactical, and everything in between. Before you can make a good decision, you need to know why it matters. What makes this decision important? Why do you need to make it? Decision objectives describe the outcomes you need to achieve as a result of making this decision.

- Is this a strategic decision that affects the overall vision, mission, and direction of your organization?
- Is it tactical, deciding on how you'll implement policy or strategy?
- Are you deciding how to build an optimal value-generating portfolio?
- Is there one overriding organizational objective that drives this decision, such as crisis prevention, disaster recovery, regulatory compliance, protecting reputation, building market share, innovation . . . ?

Without clear objectives, you can't know if your decision outcomes are good, bad, or indifferent. All objectives need to be measurable, and decision objectives are no different. Whether you use quantitative or qualitative measures for decision objectives, these will be in line with how you measure performance at an organizational level.

Clearly defined and measurable decision objectives allow you to assess the quality of your decision-making process and define metrics to track progress toward the outcomes.

2.1.2 Context

Once you know why the decision matters, defined by its objectives, you can then consider the *context* of your decision. You need to consider both external and internally driven contextual factors, looking backwards at past performance and forward to include emerging trends. This will help you to identify:

- Underlying assumptions, constraints, and/or dependencies
- Time or cost pressures
- Stakeholders who have influence and/or would be impacted
- Governance requirements

2.1.3 Options

Based on the objectives and the context, there will be alternative routes to take. You must explore the alternatives that you need to decide between and define comparable *options*. It's common to only consider a small number of apparently "obvious" options, but a good decision in a risky and important situation is likely to require creative options that address the context and objectives. Each option has associated costs, benefits, threats, and opportunities, and you need to be able to understand the implications of each, comparing them on a consistent basis. The option set must always include the "Do nothing differently" option of maintaining the status quo, with at least two other viable options. Most decisions have more than two possible options, and offering only one alternative to carrying on as normal is likely to ignore other significant possibilities.

· · · · ·

When you've defined your *decision objectives,* understood the *decision context,* and have a clear set of *decision options,* then the pieces are in place to make a good decision. But who will make it?

2.2 Decision Makers

People make decisions, and they have a huge influence on the quality and outcome of the decision-making process. This is true of the *individuals* in a decision-making group, as well as the *group* itself. Good decisions can only be made by competent individuals, but the way they function as a group is also vital. We'll explore further what we mean by competent individuals and functioning groups in Chapter 4. Here we'll focus on the people-related variables that contribute to an intelligent decision-making process.

As you work toward making a risky and important decision, you need to consider the "facts" that you assume to be stable, as well as uncertainties relating to each alternative course of action. Many decision makers approach this intuitively, basing their assumptions about what is "true" and judgments on the riskiness of each option on "gut-feel." This affects both individuals and the decision-making group.

- Each individual's personality includes *risk preferences* that influence how comfortable they feel when taking risk. Often individuals are unaware of their underlying risk preferences, and just "feel" that something is too risky or not. This feeling may result in factors being assumed to be stable when they are not, or uncertainties being discounted as improbable or insignificant.

- A stable decision-making group will have a shared view of the "right way" to address risk, reflecting their *risk culture*. This shapes the group's risk-taking behavior, including when they make risky and important decisions. Unfortunately, risk culture is intangible, making it hard to see and difficult to change. Where the decision-making group involves people from other organizations or cultures, you need to find a way to get value from the differences.

Although it is a fact that everyone has risk preferences and groups are influenced by their risk culture, these intuitive and internal factors don't always produce appropriate behavior. The *commitment to action* of the people who need to support and implement a decision is influenced by the degree to which they agree with the decision objectives, context, and option chosen. How might all of this affect our ability to make a risky and important decision?

2.3 Making the Initial Decision

The first question to ask when you need to make a risky and important decision is, "How risky is it?" Every decision has a degree of *risk*

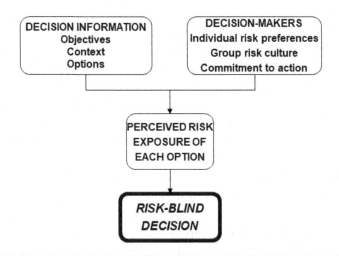

Figure 2.1   Making a Risk-Blind Decision

exposure associated with it, but the way this is viewed and understood by individuals and groups can vary. We're all affected by *risk perception*, which in turn is influenced by a wide range of factors. (We'll explore risk perception in more detail in Chapter 3.)

Both *individual risk preferences* and *group risk culture* affect perception of risk. This means that when you ask the simple question—"How risky is this decision?"—your first answer is almost always wrong! If you go ahead and make a decision at this point, based on hidden influences, the decision outcome is unlikely to take proper account of the real level of risk exposure. We describe this as a *Risk-Blind Decision,* as shown in Figure 2.1.

Making a Risk-Blind Decision involves the following steps:

- Clarifying the requirement for a decision: measurable decision goals (objectives), the situation in which you're making the decision (context), and the alternatives being considered and their implications (options)
- Determining who will make the decision (usually a decision-making group comprising a number of individuals)
- Choosing a decision option, driven by how the group perceives risk

You'll probably recognize this process! Many boards or senior teams know how to define the decision to be made, then they simply choose an option. But if asked, they would struggle to explain how their decision takes account of risk, since they are relying on intuition, gut-feel, or experience.

We describe this as a Risk-Blind Decision because there is no conscious assessment of the riskiness of the decision or the appropriateness of the result. This type of decision is influenced by unseen factors rather than consciously responding to a robust understanding of facts and risk. If you decide based on what gut-feel or intuition tells you about the riskiness of the decision, you have no way of knowing whether you've taken too much risk, or even what "too much risk" might mean.

Fortunately, it's possible to do better than making Risk-Blind Decisions.

2.4 Making a Risk-Informed Decision

The first improvement to the decision-making process illustrated in Figure 2.1 is to understand what you mean by "too much risk." This is defined by *risk thresholds*, which in turn reflect your *risk appetite*.

Risk appetite is *"the tendency of an individual or group to take risk in a given situation"* (Hillson & Murray-Webster, 2012). It's based on the risk preferences of individuals and the risk culture shared by the group. Risk appetite is an internal drive or tendency, and it can't be directly measured or managed. But we can express risk appetite through quantified risk thresholds that define the upper and lower limits of acceptable uncertainty for a particular risky decision.

The first step your decision-making group can take to improve a Risk-Blind Decision is to understand your risk appetite. Consider the objectives, context, and options for your decision, and ask yourselves how much risk you're prepared to take in order to achieve your objectives. Then quantify this using min/max risk thresholds around each objective, stating the degree of variation you're prepared to tolerate. This is easy to say and can be difficult to achieve (we'll explore this further in Chapter 7), but it's vital to make clear what is "at risk" when you take the decision.

The same process is needed to establish the appetite for risk for organization-level objectives. We'd expect that, for most risky and important decisions, the risk thresholds for the decision will be a subset of the thresholds for the organization, measured in the same way.

Once you've agreed upon the amount of risk you're prepared to take, you can now determine whether your perception of the riskiness of a particular decision option involves too much risk and choose an option that stays within the limits of the risk thresholds that you've set. We call this a *Risk-Informed Decision* because it considers risk explicitly, as shown in Figure 2.2.

This is clearly an improvement on the Risk-Blind Decision, because it reflects your view of how much risk is too much for this particular decision, allowing you to choose a decision option that lies within the chosen thresholds. But there is still something missing.

There's another way in which the amount of risk can be "too much," and that is if the risk exposure exceeds the *risk capacity* of the organization. We define risk capacity as *the amount of risk an organization as a whole is able to bear.* Imagine a situation in which you set risk thresholds to reflect your risk appetite for a decision, and you then choose a decision option that lies within those thresholds—but the amount of risk you end up taking with this option would cause major difficulties for the organization if the worst happened financially or reputationally. The model clearly needs another checkpoint to ensure that you don't select a decision option that would exceed your risk capacity.

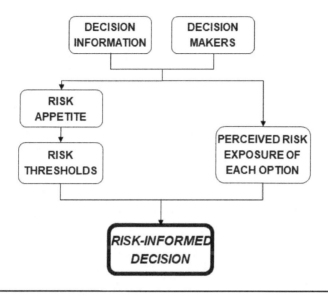

Figure 2.2   Making a Risk-Informed Decision

So, making a Risk-Informed Decision builds on the Risk-Blind Decision by taking into account the following questions:

- How much risk are you prepared to take in order to achieve your decision objectives?
  ○ This is your *risk appetite*, expressed in *risk thresholds.*
- How risky is each decision option? How confident can you be that the option you choose will work out as planned?
  ○ This is influenced by your *risk perception.*
- Which decision options lie within the risk thresholds that you set and also within the overall *risk capacity* of the organization?
  ○ These are the rational options to consider further.

2.5 Making a Risk-Intelligent Decision

The Risk-Informed Decision is based on applying risk thresholds that reflect your risk appetite. Because risk appetite is internal, it's hard to express or measure and difficult to influence. What happens if your risk appetite and the associated risk thresholds are inappropriate—either because they don't take account of all relevant information, or because

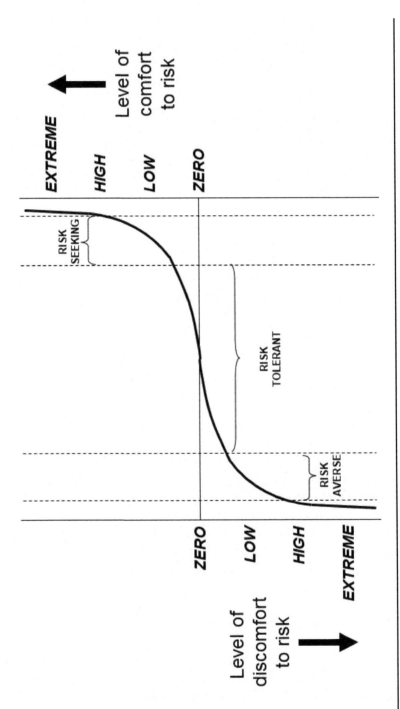

Figure 2.3 Risk Attitude Spectrum (Source: Adapted from Hillson & Murray-Webster [2007]; used with permission)

they're biased by the group involved? What happens if none of the decision options fall within the defined thresholds?

You still need to take a decision, so something has to change. One way forward is to try to manage the risk associated with one or more decision options, to produce an option that lies within the risk thresholds and the risk capacity. If this isn't possible, you need to change something else.

The only way to proceed in these circumstances is to modify your risk thresholds intentionally. But risk thresholds express your underlying risk appetite, which is an internal drive to take risk in a given situation. It's not possible to change your risk appetite, because this reflects your inherent risk-taking preferences and the risk culture of the decision-making group.

There is another way to change risk thresholds, and that's by making an *intentional choice* to do so. If you recognize that following your gut-feel risk appetite isn't helping you to make a good decision, then instead you can intervene and choose to go in a different direction.

This involves considering your *risk attitude*. Risk attitude is *"the chosen response to a given risky situation, influenced by risk perception"* (Hillson & Murray-Webster, 2012). Ultimately your risk attitude is your choice. Risk attitudes range from strongly risk averse to extreme risk seeking, as illustrated in Figure 2.3 and summarized in Table 2.1.

Different risk attitudes result in different amounts of risk taking. In each situation, you have a tendency to take risks that reflect your inherent risk appetite. But sometimes this default position can lead you to take too much or too little risk. Where this happens, you need to adopt a risk

Table 2.1 Definition of Basic Risk Attitudes

Risk Attitude	Definition
Risk averse	Uncomfortable with uncertainty, desire to avoid or reduce threats and exploit opportunities to remove uncertainty. Would be unhappy with an uncertain outcome.
Risk tolerant	Tolerant of uncertainty, no strong desire to respond to threats or opportunities in any way. Could tolerate an uncertain outcome if necessary.
Risk seeking	Comfortable with uncertainty, no desire to avoid or reduce threats or to exploit opportunities to remove uncertainty. Would be happy with an uncertain outcome.

Source: Adapted from Murray-Webster & Hillson (2008), used with permission.

attitude that will moderate your risk-taking behavior to something more appropriate in the situation. We'll cover how to do this in Chapter 5.

Changing risk attitude leads to a change in risk thresholds, as you intentionally choose to take more or less risk in the decision. This provides a control point in the decision-making process. Figure 2.4 shows how we can modify the Risk-Informed Decision to include this control point, with the following steps:

- Choosing an attitude toward risk taking which maximizes the chances of achieving the decision objectives and which also remains within the organizational risk capacity.
- Modifying risk thresholds to reflect the degree of risk taking that matches your chosen risk attitude.
- Considering each decision option, choosing the option that lies within the modified risk thresholds and where there is the greatest commitment to action. If no option is suitable, you may need to choose a different risk attitude.

A control loop is provided by this sequence of: choose risk attitude ⇨ modify risk thresholds ⇨ consider decision options. This loop should be repeated until the perceived risk exposure of at least one decision option falls within risk thresholds.

We call this a Risk-Intelligent Decision because it reflects:

- The decision objectives, context, options, and commitment to action
- Individual risk preferences and shared risk culture
- Perception of the degree of risk exposure associated with each decision option
- Explicit consideration of risk appetite, expressed in risk thresholds
- A chosen risk attitude that maximizes the chances of achieving decision objectives

The model in Figure 2.4 links the factors impacting risky and important decisions, providing a robust basis for making intelligent decisions that take account of all the variables, with a control loop to ensure that the risk thresholds applied to the decision are appropriate to the risk exposure in the decision context.

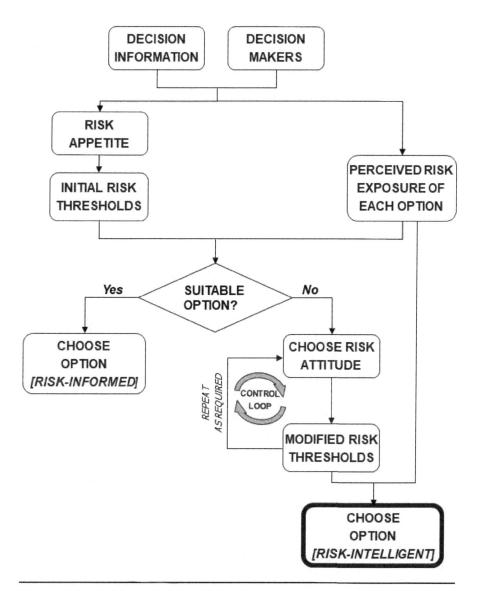

Figure 2.4 Making a Risk-Intelligent Decision

We recognize that the work required to adopt a risk-intelligent decision-making process could be significant. But if the decision you're making is risky and important, can you afford not to invest the time and effort to get it right?

2.6 Key Points

In this chapter, we've discovered the following:

1. Before making a decision, you need to understand both the decision information (objectives, context, and options) and the decision makers (especially their individual risk preferences, shared risk culture, and commitment to action).
2. To make a risky and important decision, you need to know the level of risk associated with each decision option. This is driven by risk perception, which may not be reliable.
3. You also need to know how much risk is tolerable. This requires you to understand your risk appetite and express it in measurable risk thresholds, then choose a decision option that lies within the thresholds.
4. If no decision option falls below risk thresholds, it's possible to choose a different risk attitude and modify thresholds accordingly.

2.7 Looking Forward

In Chapter 3, we delve deeper into the factors that influence risk perception for you, for your colleagues, and for the decision-making group as a whole.

References

Hillson, D. A., and Murray-Webster, R. (2007). *Understanding and Managing Risk Attitude*, 2nd edition. Aldershot, UK: Gower.

Hillson, D. A., and Murray-Webster, R. (2012). *A Short Guide to Risk Appetite*. Aldershot, UK: Gower.

Murray-Webster, R., and Hillson, D. A. (2008). *Managing Group Risk Attitude*. Aldershot, UK: Gower.

Chapter 3

Perception Is Reality

Risk perception lies at the center of the Risk-Intelligent Decision model that we developed in the previous chapter (see Figure 2.4). We define risk perception as *the way risk is viewed, understood, and interpreted by an individual or a group.* Our decision is shaped by how decision *objectives* and *context* are interpreted through our perception. Decision *options* and the implications of these on objectives are judged through the same perceptual filters. Our *commitment to action* is greater when the option matches our intuition of whether the chosen option makes good sense or not.

A well-known saying tells us that, "Perception is reality" (though no one is sure who really said it!). More specifically, Edward de Bono said, "Perception is real, even when it is not reality" (de Bono, 1969).

This clearly matters when you are making a risky and important decision. You can't know for sure precisely how risky each decision element really is. Instead you have to rely on your perception of its riskiness. And it's at this point that you have a problem. We hinted at this in the previous chapter, when we described risk perception as "influenced by a wide range of factors." Here we explore what those influences are and why they matter to risky decision making.

3.1 Influences on Perception

We divide the influences on risk perception into three groups we call the "triple strand," which is made up of conscious factors, subconscious factors, and affective factors (see Figure 3.1). While the three strands overlap and interact in complex ways, it is helpful to separate them so that we can examine and understand them properly. The following paragraphs consider each strand in turn, and Table 3.1 presents examples.

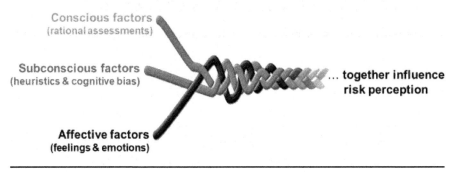

Figure 3.1   The Triple Strand of Influences on Risk Perception (*Source:* Adapted from Hillson & Murray-Webster [2007], used with permission)

Table 3.1 Examples of Triple-Strand Influences

Conscious Factors	Subconscious Factors		Affective Factors
	Heuristics	Cognitive Biases	
Potential benefit	Representativeness	Propinquity	Fear
Urgency	Availability	Illusion of control	Desire
Proximity	Confirmation trap	Illusion of knowledge	Love
Impact range	Anchoring	Intelligence trap	Hatred
Manageability	Groupthink	Optimism bias	Joy
Experience	Cultural conformity	Precautionary principle	Sadness
	Risky/cautious shift	Loss aversion	Anger
	Follow the leader		Shame
	Lure of choice		

3.1.1 Conscious Factors

These are situational characteristics of a particular risky and important decision that you can observe, count, and measure, and that you can describe and assess in a rational way despite the presence of uncertainty. This is the realm of facts and figures, data and information, probabilities and predictions.

You are likely aware of this type of factor, and you are comfortable using conscious factors when you make risky decisions. They include questions that have numerical or quantifiable answers, such as, "How many? How much? How long? Who? When?" Some conscious factors can be analyzed using standard techniques such as cost–benefit analysis, discounted cashflow, internal rate of return, hurdle rates, payback periods, market share, profitability, return on investment, real options analysis, and so on. Others can be counted or verified through documented evidence.

It's natural for you to use conscious factors when considering the riskiness of a decision situation and how risky each decision option might be. These factors are well known and understood, and on the face of it everyone knows what they mean and how to use them. It's easy to trust these factors because they seem to be rational, explicit, and based on conscious thought. Unfortunately, they are not the only factors that influence your risk perception. The other two parts of the triple strand also affect the way you view risk, and it's unwise to ignore their influences.

3.1.2 Subconscious Factors

These factors lie below the level of conscious or rational awareness, which means that they're likely to be missed unless you know they're there. Despite operating in the subconscious realm, these factors have a powerful effect on how riskiness is viewed. You need to understand them so that you can determine whether their influence is helping or hindering a balanced decision. By becoming aware of subconscious factors, you can choose to correct for any bias or inaccuracies that they introduce into your decision making.

Subconscious factors fall into two groups: heuristics and cognitive biases.

- *Heuristics* are mental short-cuts or rules of thumb based on previous experience. Your brain uses them to make rapid sense of complex or uncertain situations when there isn't time or data to make a rational assessment. They generally operate by comparing the situation that you're currently facing with things you've seen before. This is fine when the basis for the comparison is accurate. But because heuristics operate subconsciously, it's not possible to check whether their influence is correct or not. Often a heuristic is a valid way of reaching a conclusion quickly and accurately, saving the effort of consciously assessing the situation at hand. But sometimes your brain uses a heuristic that doesn't apply or isn't relevant, resulting in an influence that's not appropriate.

- *Cognitive biases* are inbuilt systematic ways of thinking which deviate from the norm. Unlike heuristics, which might be helpful or not, cognitive biases always lead to an incorrect result. They introduce a tendency toward a particular way of thinking which is not necessarily rational. This means that cognitive biases will skew your risk perception one way or another, based on underlying beliefs that are untrue, inaccurate, or irrelevant.

3.1.3 Affective Factors

The third part of the triple strand is an area that makes many senior leaders uncomfortable. Affective factors are gut-level visceral feelings and emotions which arise automatically or instinctively in a situation. They make you react without thinking, making you literally irrational. Your emotions are automatically triggered when you experience a situation that is the same or similar to something that's happened before.

Many professionals believe that their decision making is dispassionate, fact-based, rational, and grounded. The sad yet true fact is that everyone's emotional state colors the way they view the situation within which they're trying to make a decision. This affects judgments on objectives, context, options and commitment to action.

Emotions can arise as a direct result of the decision context. For example, you might be *cross* with a member of your team, *frustrated* at the lack of time or data to make the decision, or *worried* about the potential of making a wrong decision. You might be *excited* by the prospect of unlocking a difficult situation, or *enjoying* the challenge of creating a new business opportunity. Each of these emotional states will influence your ability to make a fully rational choice.

But you might also be experiencing emotions from situations outside the decision-making context, or even outside work itself. Feelings of *grief, depression, elation,* or *joy* from your personal life affect your mood and the way you approach the task of decision making. Such feelings can be particularly influential when the decision is uncertain or risky and when there's a lot riding on the outcome.

In some cultures the myth still exists that, "Good leaders don't have feelings," and this may be reinforced by national and societal norms. Despite the assertion, emotional state has a strong influence on perception, and therefore on your ability to make good decisions. Leaders are real people with real feelings. How might your own emotions be affecting the way you make risky decisions?

3.2 Understanding the Strands

Risk perception is influenced by each of the three parts of the triple strand, and the way you make risky and important decisions is driven by your perception of the riskiness of the decision situation and associated decision options. In such situations it's vital for you to understand what's influencing your risk perception and to make adjustments for any unhelpful influences. This means understanding and managing the various parts of the triple strand. Let's look at each in a little more detail, working through the examples in Table 3.1.

3.2.1 Conscious Factors

This is the area in which many decision makers are most comfortable. All conscious factors are explicit and measurable, and well-established methods and models are used for analysis. This makes them easy to understand and to accept as being reliable. Estimates are required, of course, and these will never be precisely correct, but techniques are available for you to establish confidence levels. You may not like the results of an analysis, but you rarely challenge the way they were produced.

Because conscious factors can be observed and determined, and most of them can be quantified, you can take account of their importance when you consider how risky each decision option might be. Examples of *conscious factors* include (Table 3.1):

- **Potential benefit/return.** What are the benefits from selecting this decision option? How much might you increase market share or share price? What increased revenue might result? What is the return on investment, internal rate of return, payback period?

- **Urgency.** How quickly do you need to make this decision? Are any of the options time sensitive? What is your window of opportunity to act? Do you have days, weeks, months, or years to make your decision?
- **Proximity.** How much time do you have before any risks associated with this decision option might occur? If a risk occurs, would it be sooner or later?
- **Impact range.** If the risks linked to this course of action happened, what kind of effect would you expect (remembering that some risks can have bad impacts, while others can be positively helpful)? How big might the impact be in financial or reputational terms?
- **Manageability.** If one or more risks actually happened, how easily could you deal with it? You can assess manageability on a scale from 1 to 5, ranging from impossible to easy, allowing it to form part of your rational determination of riskiness. Assessment of manageability is likely to be influenced by experience.
- **Experience.** How many times have you done this before (successfully or not)? How many years of combined relevant experience does the team have?

The influence of conscious factors on your decision is clear for all to see. Nothing is hidden, so your team or decision-making group can discuss each factor sensibly, weighing different factors against one another to make a rational choice on the best way forward.

So far, so good. This is the easy part of the triple strand. The problem is that visible, quantifiable, rational, situational factors are not the only influences on your decision. You also need to take account of the other two strands, which are hidden and not immediately available for conscious analysis.

3.2.2 Subconscious Factors

These fall under two headings: *heuristics* and *cognitive biases*. Both of these operate below the radar of consciousness, so you need to look out for them intentionally and address them proactively whenever you spot one in operation.

We'll come back to handling heuristics and correcting cognitive biases in Chapter 5. Before you can manage them, you need to understand them. A lot has been written elsewhere about these factors, so we'll briefly describe the key ones here.

There are many subconscious heuristics, some of which affect individuals, while others operate within groups. Heuristics help you make rapid assessments when you don't have sufficient time or data to make a more considered judgment. Sometimes they are accurate and helpful, but not always. Your decision making won't be affected by all of these all of the time, but some of them will definitely be influential in each risky and important decision. The key is to discover which ones, to be aware of their effects, and to counter them where possible. The main heuristics include the following (see Table 3.1 and Figure 3.2):

- **Representativeness.** This occurs when you think the situation that you're currently facing is like one you've seen before, and therefore the level of riskiness will be similar. For example, in Figure 3.2, when you're trying to assess the "octagon" situation, the closest fit from your previous experience is the "circle," so you subconsciously assume that the current situation will be similar.
- **Availability.** It's easier for you to recall things that are either recent or dramatic or both. When your subconscious is looking for a reference point against which to compare the riskiness of the current situation, you'll tend to overemphasize the relevance of recent major events. In Figure 3.2, events that are closer in time or higher in significance appear subconsciously to be more important.
- **Confirmation trap.** If you already think you know the answer, your subconscious selects supportive evidence to reinforce your prior view, even if contradictory evidence is stronger. The figure shows opposing evidence being subconsciously blocked, leaving only data that confirm your existing view.
- **Anchoring.** When you think you know the answer or you already have something in mind, your subconscious tends to start with that value and then adjust from it, rather than allowing you to make a fresh assessment. Figure 3.2 shows how varying from an initial anchor value subconsciously prevents you from considering all possible values.
- **Groupthink.** If everyone else in your decision-making group expresses an opinion, you tend to follow the crowd and agree, even

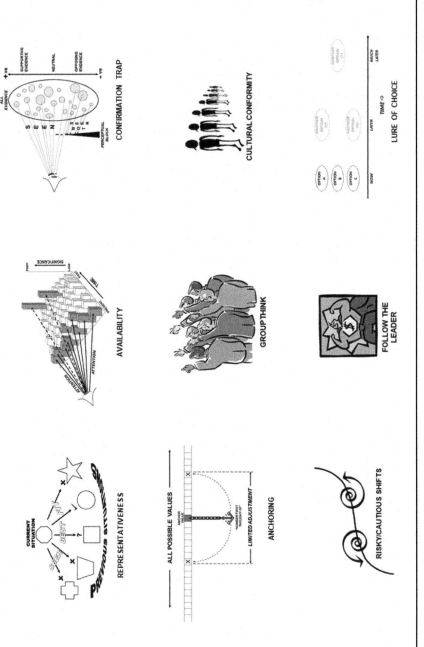

Figure 3.2 Illustrations of Heuristics (*Source:* Adapted from Hillson & Murray-Webster [2007], used with permission)

against your better judgment. The majority say it's like this, and your subconscious doesn't allow you to differ.

- **Cultural conformity.** When your organization or group has a strong culture with clear expectations, your subconscious prefers to be aligned with cultural norms. This can suppress your personal opinion, depriving the decision-making process of your input.
- **Risky/cautious shift.** When individuals are in a group, they tend to take more extreme positions than they would on their own. This subconscious influence can drive you to take more risk than you're comfortable with (a risky shift) or less (a cautious shift). In Figure 3.2, these shifts are shown as movements up or down the risk attitude spectrum, toward more or less risk-taking positions.
- **Follow the leader.** When you're in a group with a strong leader, you subconsciously tend to match their position, adopting the same or similar view of how risky a situation is. This can be particularly influential when the leader is charismatic, experienced, or older.
- **Lure of choice.** This heuristic is based on the idea that a better option might turn up later, so your subconscious favours delay over making an immediate choice. Figure 3.2 shows how the possibility of other options down the line can make you uncomfortable in choosing now between the options that are actually before you.

The first four of these heuristics (representativeness, availability, confirmation trap, anchoring) tend to influence individuals; the next four (groupthink, cultural conformity, risky/cautious shift, follow the leader) are more applicable to groups; and the last (lure of choice) can influence both individuals and groups.

In addition to these heuristics, your perception of the riskiness of a situation or decision option will be affected by various subconscious cognitive biases (listed in Table 3.1). Like heuristics, these won't all be relevant to you in a particular situation, but you'll make better decisions if you know which ones are influencing your perception. The main cognitive biases include:

- **Propinquity.** This term refers to how close you are to the issue being considered and how much it matters to you personally. High propinquity may make you either more cautious or more adventurous about something.

- **Illusion of control.** This bias leads you to believe that you are more in control of events than you really are, and it can cause you to take more risk than you would normally.
- **Illusion of knowledge.** This is a sense that you "should know" more about the situation than you really do, and it leads to a higher sense of confidence than is justified.
- **Intelligence trap.** If you believe that you are intelligent and have verbal fluency, your ability to argue your point of view can produce overconfidence in the validity of your perceptions.
- **Optimism bias.** This mindset drives you to discount risk on the assumption that things are more likely to go well for you than for the average person.
- **Precautionary principle.** This bias is typified by the phrase, "Better safe than sorry," leading you to be more cautious than perhaps you should be.
- **Loss aversion.** This is the tendency to prefer avoiding losses to acquiring equivalent gains. For individuals, the pain of losing is psychologically more acute than the pleasure of gaining.

3.2.3 Affective Factors

This is perhaps the hardest strand to handle when you make risky decisions, because it relates to your inner world of feelings and emotions. Some people like to think that everyone should leave their emotions behind when considering a work decision, and that effective decision makers are dispassionate, driven only by facts and data. Some consider that people who bring their passions to work are irrational and ineffective in decision-making situations. We've already seen that there are many hidden subconscious factors at work to influence your perception of risk. In addition to these, your internal emotional environment has a significant effect. Whether we like this or not, we ignore it at our peril.

We tend to think of emotions as fluffy and ill-defined, but organizational psychologists and others tell a different story. René Descartes wrote *Les Passions de l'âme* in 1649, in which he described six "passions of the soul": wonder, love, hatred, desire, joy, sadness. Descartes believed that all other emotions are either subspecies of these six or combinations of them. Other thinkers add fear, anger, and shame to this list.

Whichever emotions we include, it's important to recognize that your emotional state affects the choices you make. This includes emotions that have arisen outside the workplace which have no apparent connection with the decision you're trying to make—except that you yourself are the connection. Without conscious control, you bring your emotions with you to the decision-making table.

Emotions in the office can affect many different elements of the work experience, but they are particularly influential when you're making risky decisions. They include the following (see Table 3.1):

- **Fear.** You may experience this emotion as worry, concern, or anxiety about something, or it might be as strong as feeling dread. You may be concerned about some aspect of the decision, or you could be worrying about the situation at home or with a family member. Maybe a health issue is causing anxiety, or something is threatening your reputation. When you're experiencing these emotions, your perception of risk will be heightened, leading you to be more cautious and protective.
- **Desire.** This emotion can also appear as excitement, wonder, curiosity, or inquisitiveness. You may have a new interest outside work, which could include a hobby or sport. These positive feelings can influence you toward taking more risk, driven by the desire more than by concern over potential pitfalls or hazards.
- **Love.** There are many different levels of intensity for this emotion, ranging from attraction through romantic involvement to lust or obsession. Love produces a positive emotional environment that influences your perception of almost everything, and it makes you tend toward seeing the good in every situation.
- **Hatred.** The opposite of love, hatred exists in less extreme versions which include dislike, disrespect, criticism, or scepticism. When you're feeling one of these emotions either inside or outside the work setting, it will influence you toward choices that reinforce your wish to protect yourself and deny satisfaction to someone else.
- **Joy.** This positive emotion has many expressions, including happiness, optimism, being carefree, etc. You might describe a joyful person as "happy-go-lucky," which indicates their tendency to believe that things will go their way, so they may be more comfortable taking risk.

- **Sadness.** If you feel sad for any reason, it can affect your willingness to engage with the decision process, and it may make you especially unprepared to take risk. Sadness includes grief, depression, and angst, and it is a powerful influence on those who feel it.
- **Anger.** While it is generally considered unacceptable to express unmitigated anger in a work setting, it's still possible to be feeling angry inside, either justifiably or for no good reason. Degrees of anger can range from mild irritation to blind rage. It's hard to make a rational decision while you are angry with someone, something, or some situation, and any choice you make is likely to be skewed in one direction or another.
- **Shame.** If you feel ashamed, you may either disqualify yourself from making a decision, preferring to withdraw and be as invisible as possible, or perhaps you may choose to behave in a way to justify yourself instead. You may not have the confidence to say what you think, and you will treat your contribution as being of little value or likely to be ignored by others. Shame, which often arises from a sense of isolation or discrimination, can alternatively result in over-assertiveness or indignant or self-righteous behaviors.

3.3 Reconstructing the Triple Strand

Each of the three strands is important, because each influences your perception of the risk associated with the decision objectives, decision context, decision options, and your commitment to action. We could try to address each strand separately, but they don't exist or operate in isolation in reality. Instead, they are interwoven to form a complex set of influences (as shown in Figure 3.1). You might think that you've made a rational assessment of the situation and decided on a particular option based on conscious factors, but your assessment will have been shaped by subconscious heuristics and sources of cognitive bias, and your judgment will be colored by your current underlying emotions.

The triple strand influences your risk perception in two important ways: it affects how risky you think something is, and it shapes what you think is the right way to respond. When you understand how each part of the triple strand drives your perception of risk, you can manage it proactively and improve the way you make risky and important decisions. In Chapter 5 we'll provide a simple framework to help you respond to triple-strand influences, including the hidden areas of subconscious and affective factors.

3.4 Key Points

In this chapter we discussed what influences your perception of risk, which in turn drives the way you make risky decisions. This chapter has shown that:

1. You can't "know" how risky something is—it's based on your perception of the level of risk. But risk perception is influenced by many factors, and it may not be a reliable indicator of riskiness.
2. The triple strand groups influences on risk perception into three categories: conscious (rational assessments), subconscious (heuristics and cognitive biases), and affective (gut-level feelings and emotions). You need to understand these before you can take account of them.
3. The triple strand of influences impact individuals and groups.
4. Each strand needs to be understood so you can unpick the combined effect.

3.5 Looking Forward

Chapter 4 considers the people involved in making risky and important decisions. We provide a framework for considering the competence of individuals, and we examine the features of effective decision-making groups.

References

de Bono, E. (1969). *The Mechanism of Mind*. London, UK: Jonathan Cape.
Descartes, R. (1649). *Les Passions de l'âme*. Paris, France: chez Henry Le Gras.
Hillson, D. A., and Murray-Webster, R. (2007). *Understanding and Managing Risk Attitude*, 2nd edition. Aldershot, UK: Gower.

Chapter 4

Value from Difference

The Risk-Intelligent Decision model we built in Chapter 2 has risk perception at its center, and we saw in the last chapter that there are many influences on how you perceive risk. These affect you as an individual, but there are also factors that drive the way groups see risk.

Clearly, if you want to make good decisions in risky and important situations, it's vital that you get the people issues right. This includes having *individuals who are competent to make decisions*, as well as *decision-making groups that are functioning effectively*. What do we mean by competent individuals and functioning groups?

4.1 Competent Individuals

It sounds obvious to say that good decisions can only be made by competent individuals. But how do you know if someone is competent?

4.1.1 Defining Competence

Competence is the ability to do a specific task or role effectively, measured in terms of behavior and performance that can be observed in practice. In this case, we're looking for individuals who are competent at making risky and important decisions. We define five elements of competence using our PEAKS Framework (Murray-Webster & Hillson, 2002), as illustrated in Table 4.1:

Table 4.1 Definitions of PEAKS Elements

PEAKS Element	Description
Personal characteristics	Personal characteristics are *natural preferences and traits*. These tend to form the basis of a person's style and natural reactions to situations. Some may change over time through personal development or gaining experience, but in general they are not easily influenced by traditional training.
Experience	Experience must be *acquired*, not only in formal paid jobs, but also from other life contexts. Experience does not simply equate to time spent in a particular environment but is measured by relevant achievements. The assessment of experience will always be *relative to the needs of a specific organizational requirement*.
Attitudes	Attitudes are *chosen responses* to situations. Some attitudes may be deeply rooted, representing core values for that individual, but they nevertheless represent a choice. Other attitudes may be more malleable. Attitudes differ from personal characteristics in that they are situational responses rather than natural preferences or traits, and different attitudes may therefore be chosen depending on the context.
Knowledge	Knowledge is *learned, often theoretically via traditional training, or can be gained on the job*. It includes familiarity with the widely-held principles about a particular subject and the way those principles should be applied to best effect.
Skills	Skills are also learned, but must be *developed experientially*. They are more accurately described as being the skillful application of P, E, A, and K as described above.

Source: Based on Murray-Webster & Hillson (2002), used with permission.

- Personal characteristics (Who am I?)
- Experience (What have I done previously?)
- Attitudes (How do I choose to respond?)
- Knowledge (What do I know?)
- Skills (How ably can I apply my experience, attitudes, and knowledge?)

4.1.2 Competent Decision Making

PEAKS is a generic competence framework that can be applied to any task or role. Each of the five PEAKS elements can be described in more detail using a set of attributes. If you want to use PEAKS in practice to ensure that your decision-making group is made up of competent individuals, you need to develop a specific set of PEAKS attributes that describes the elements of competent decision making. This requires you to answer the following questions:

P: What kind of person would help us to make a good decision?

E: What experience must they have had in order to be able to contribute positively?

A: Which attitudes would support us in making a good decision, and which would hinder?

K: What must they know in order to understand the decision that we're making and make a positive contribution to the decision process?

S: What skills will they need in order to help us make our decision?

Table 4.2 provides some examples of the attributes you might be looking for in the individuals who make up your decision-making group (including yourself). These are just for illustration, and you'll need to review and customize them in order to cover the specific areas of competence relevant to your business. You won't need all of these attributes in every decision-making setting of course, and you're really unlikely to find them all in one person. But you need to understand what makes

Table 4.2 Example Attributes for Each PEAKS Element

PEAKS Element	Example Attributes
Personal Characteristics	• At ease with making decisions • Tolerance for ambiguity and change • Enjoys problem solving • Pragmatic • Self-aware, self-confident, self-sustaining • Intuitive and sensitive to the needs of others • Adaptable in behavior and approach • Emotionally resilient

(Continued on following page)

Table 4.2 Example Attributes for Each PEAKS Element (*Continued*)

PEAKS Element	Example Attributes
Experience	• Decision making in similar contexts • Operating within relevant legal constraints • Meeting relevant regulatory standards • Balancing competing stakeholder needs • Performing/interpreting strategic and business analysis • Understanding and using risk-based data and information • Problem-solving techniques • Negotiation and conflict resolution • Working in teams • Applying relevant policies and procedures
Attitudes	• Committed to integrity, transparency, and honesty • Prioritizes organizational needs over personal agenda • Supportive of organization values and desired culture • Concerned to meet stakeholder needs • Team player, willing to trust and respect others • Possibility thinker ("can-do" attitude) • Willing to reflect and be challenged • Assertive (win/win approach) • Prepared to take appropriate risks for realistic gain • Willing to commit to action to implement shared and agreed decision outcomes
Knowledge	• Specific decision objectives, context, and options • Decision-making processes • Awareness of heuristics and cognitive biases • Decision analysis techniques (e.g., scenario planning, horizon scanning, cost–benefit analysis, real options, multi-attribute analysis, etc.) • Risk appetite, risk thresholds, and risk capacity • Stakeholder management • Relevant regulatory and legal frameworks • Negotiation and conflict management • Communication needs and methods • Measuring performance and business benefits
Skills	• Applying an effective decision-making process • Clear and relevant communication • Behavioral flexibility • Applied emotional literacy for self and others • Exerting appropriate influence • Managing information • Critical thinking • Conflict resolution • Cultural awareness and literacy • Facilitation

a competent individual in your particular decision setting, then try to ensure that all these attributes are represented in the group of people making the decision. This may involve selecting new members for a particular decision to augment the overall team competencies.

It's important for an individual to have the right set of attributes under each PEAKS element if they are to be truly competent, and problems can occur if one or more attributes are missing. Imagine someone who has all the required knowledge, experience, and skills, but they have a negative attitude or personal characteristics that do not pre-dispose them to be effective in the situation. This person might not work well in the team environment of a decision-making group. Another person might have a positive attitude and extensive knowledge, but no relevant experience or demonstrable skills in decision making.

4.1.3 Using the PEAKS Framework

If governance arrangements allow you to make the decision alone, first try some self-examination, using the PEAKS Framework as a guide. Do you have what it takes to make this decision, in terms of experience, knowledge, skills, etc.? If not, then is there something you can do to become competent in the available time (e.g., acquire some new knowledge or choose a different attitude)? If not, you should consider involving others in a decision-making group.

When you're putting together a group to make a risky and important decision, think about what competencies are required. What kind of people do you need to include? What experience and knowledge will they need in order to make a good decision? Are there any particular attitudes that you want them to possess, and what attitudes would be unhelpful in the group? Although it would be natural for you to choose people who are like you, there is significant value in working with others who are different, because difference enables challenge, promotes creativity, and enhances value. Paraphrasing the quote attributed to William Wrigley, Jr., in 1931, *"When two people always agree, one of them is unnecessary"* (The Quotations Page: Quote from William Wrigley Jr., 2020).

Sometimes you won't be able to choose who is in your decision-making group, but it's still helpful to consider the competencies of the individuals on your core team, in case you need to bring others to create a functioning group.

4.2 Functioning Groups

It's clear that the individuals making a decision will have a major impact on decision quality. But the way they interact as a group is also important. Before you can make a good decision, you need to understand how the decision-making group functions together.

We use the term *decision-making group* here to reflect that not all risky and important decisions are made by established teams. For example, major investment decisions may involve people from multiple organizations working together for the first time. In using the term *group*, we acknowledge that it is highly desirable for the decision-making group to behave as a team—mutually accountable and committed to a common

Table 4.3 Factors Influencing the Perception of Decision-Making Groups

Group Characteristic	Description
Propinquity	Propinquity is about closeness and describes how much the decision outcome matters to the group. Leaders must understand propinquity levels and address them explicitly.
Power	Performance of the group is affected by the relative power between various individuals. Leaders should be aware of this and aim to reduce any unhelpful influence.
Group dynamics	Group dynamics influence belonging, social influence, and subsequent behaviors, including expressed perceptions of risk. They need to be actively managed to ensure optimal behavior.
Team maturity	Decision quality is influenced by the maturity of the group. Newly formed groups will behave differently from those that are more familiar and settled. A familiar and settled group is not always an indicator of maturity and effectiveness.
Leadership style	Leadership styles vary on a spectrum from dictatorial to facilitative. Leaders need to choose a style that is appropriate to the decision context.
Organizational culture	Culture has the potential to influence any of the other characteristics above. Understanding the prevailing culture helps in predicting likely behaviors. Leaders are responsible for establishing the appropriate risk culture, relevant to making risky and important decisions.

purpose, goals, and approach. However, you cannot assume that they will act like a team, and so you'll need to proceed with that in mind.

Unpicking the triple strand of influences on perception as described in the previous chapter is complex enough for individuals. When a group is involved, the perceptions of the group are not some sort of average perception. Additional factors come into play with the potential to seriously skew the rationality of the decision-making process. These factors are presented in Table 4.3, and include:

- Propinquity
- Power
- Group dynamics
- Team maturity
- Leadership style
- Organizational culture

4.2.1 Propinquity

When considering the members of the decision-making group, including yourself, the question to ask is "Who cares the most?"—who has the biggest stake? the most to gain or lose? To understand the influence of propinquity on individuals, the motto of the British Special Air Service (SAS) "Who dares wins" can be adjusted to "Who cares wins" or at least, "Who cares the most, fights hardest for what they want." This is closely related to the affective emotions part of the triple strand for individuals. Taking this idea and applying it to the group, one potential major source of bias is the degree to which your group cares about the decision objectives or one of the decision options.

Two examples might be:

- The organization is in significant trouble, and the decision is about investing very scarce resources to try to maintain a foothold in the market. The decision-making group is made up of all shareholders in the organization. The influence of their stake may drive a cautious shift as, in trying to protect what they have, they talk one another into a more risk-averse attitude than is logical in the situation.

- One member of the decision-making group has invested lots of time and effort working up their preferred option. Although not intending to create a conflict of interest, the person is so committed to their option that they are not able to consider alternatives logically. If the person is also highly verbally fluent, the effect of propinquity and the biasing effect of the intelligence trap could be highly influential.

This last example is one of the reasons we recommend that you have a minimum of two viable options in addition to the "do nothing differently" option—to prevent an individual or an alliance within the decision-making group from having the opportunity to present selective information.

The effect of propinquity of an individual on the whole group is also compounded by power levels.

4.2.2 Power

In 1960, French and Raven described five bases of power:

- **Legitimate power:** The position of power that provides a formal right to decide and to expect that others will comply if asked
- **Reward power:** The ability to compensate others for their compliance
- **Coercive power:** The belief by others that they could be punished for non-compliance
- **Expert power:** Derived from having a scarce skill or knowledge in the group
- **Referent power:** Derived from a person's attractiveness or worthiness of respect

Since then two other forms of power have been recognized in addition to the original five:

- **Informational power:** The ability to control the information that others need to accomplish something
- **Connection power:** The power that comes from having highly developed social networks and therefore the ability to call upon others to form alliances or generally help to achieve a particular outcome

None of these power bases are negative *per se*, but there can be a fine line between influence/persuasion and manipulation/bullying as group members try to cajole other members of the group down their preferred path.

The combination of high power and high propinquity provides both the motive and the means for you or another member of the group to get their own way, irrespective of whether your/their preferred way forward is logical given the hidden influences on your perception.

In established decision-making groups, power bases are well understood. As a leader, your challenge is to acknowledge the sources of power that exist, including your own, and to try to stop established power plays from biasing a robust discussion about the decision objectives, context, options, and commitment to action.

This is a key area in which your influence on the risk culture can create a context for decision making that is curious and challenging, yet respectful of others.

Both propinquity and power are features of individuals with a direct impact on the group. The next two factors influencing the perception of decision-making groups are features of the group itself.

4.2.3 Group Dynamics

These are the psychological and sociological processes that separate the workings of a group from a random collection of individuals.

We are social animals, and although you or others in the group may be very comfortable leading from the front and taking a stand, we are nevertheless inherently motivated to coordinate, adapt, and cooperate in social groups.

This is all good until the desire for cooperation, consensus, and unanimity becomes greater than the desire to make the right decision in the circumstances. Groupthink (Janis, 1972), highlighted as a subconscious heuristic in Chapter 3, is a highly influential group bias on perception of risk and decision making. Made famous after the research into the Kennedy government decision that led to the Cuban missile crisis and the invasion of the Bay of Pigs in 1963, groupthink works subconsciously, promoting the "in-group," suppressing dissenting voices and resulting in inadequate evaluation of situations and poor decisions. The saying "safety in numbers" is relevant. On the one hand, it is good for you as a leader to be able to say that the group unanimously decided this was the best way forward. On the other hand, it's a disaster if none of the group members individually would have chosen that option.

As a leader, this influence alone justifies using a neutral facilitator during evaluation of options for risky and important decisions. A trusted and skilled facilitator will respectfully expose or bypass individual and group biases and ensure that the group considers multiple alternative points of view. Be careful to give the facilitator the permission to act independently rather than as your agent, unless your objective is to get your own way!

Another aspect of group dynamics is the process that groups go through to develop maturity.

4.2.4 Team Maturity

Much has been written about high-performing teams over recent years. The Tuckman (1965, 1977) cycle of norming, storming, forming, performing, and mourning is well understood and is highly relevant to making decisions in risky and important situations. It provides a description of the stages in team development, suggesting that a mature team achieves and maintains the performing stage. However, this performing stage is rarely reached even in groups of people who have worked together for many years. Performing requires challenge, creative conflict, and the busting of the "norms" that come from a group that has just slipped into routine ways of working that are never varied or challenged.

Some behaviors become so embedded in routines that groups are totally ineffective, and group decision making is a ritual that ticks all the boxes for comfort and cohesion, but fails to consider what is needed in a mature way. This is a particular risk in decision-making groups in which the context for the decision—usually a meeting—is a formal part of governance. The Risk-Intelligent Decision is easily sacrificed for sticking to the timing on the agenda or not wanting to upset the chair in some organizations.

Recognizing such situations, current thinking in corporate governance focuses on the effectiveness of board dynamics as well as demographics, structures, and individual competencies (Cross, 2013). Board effectiveness evaluation exercises are increasingly common as a way of shining a light on the psychological and sociological influences on decision making.

So, team maturity is a both a blessing and a curse for Risk-Intelligent Decision making. If you have a decision-making group that is also a high-performing team, you are likely blessed by working with people who will put in their own challenge and adopt the behaviors that enable true evaluation of all relevant options. If not, you will need to find a way of creating an environment for this to happen. Again, expert facilitation can help you enormously, but there are things that you can do to encourage others to have an equal voice, to carve out the air time for the quieter members of the group, and to encourage others to shut up and listen.

To do this, you will need to adopt a leadership style that is more facilitative than dictatorial.

4.2.5 Leadership Style

A range of facilitative leadership styles are possible, and these vary by the amount of control exercised by the leader compared with the degree of control allowed for the group. Figure 4.1 illustrates the facilitation spectrum, which shows a continuous range of the balance between leader control and group control. On the far left-hand side, the leader has almost complete control over what happens in the decision-making meeting. By contrast, on the far right-hand side, the group has near total control of the proceedings. Between these extremes lie various shared positions in which the balance of control differs between leader and group.

Although the facilitation spectrum is a continuous range, it is helpful to distinguish three general zones. In the left-hand area, the leader takes charge with a *directive* style, while the group is in *reactive* mode, following

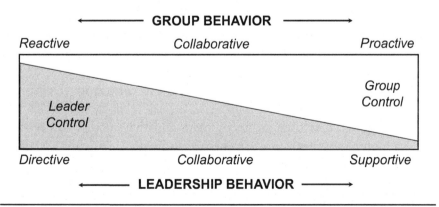

Figure 4.1   The Facilitation Spectrum (*Source:* Based on Hillson [2015], used with permission)

the leader. The right-hand zone sees the group operating in a *proactive* manner, with the leader in a *supportive* role. Between these two lies a central region in which both leader and group are in *collaborative* mode, working together to achieve the best outcomes from the meeting.

Having recognized that an effective leader can operate in a range of different styles, this raises an important question: When should you use each style? Different styles are appropriate at different points in a decision-making meeting, and a skillful leader will be able to select the right style for the changing situation.

For example, it might be appropriate to be directive at the beginning of the meeting, to give a clear start by clarifying decision objectives and options, defining the agenda and setting ground rules. You might also want to be directive when summarizing outcomes and clarifying next steps as the meeting closes. You could adopt alternative styles in the middle part of the meeting, depending on the maturity and experience of the people involved, both in terms of the background of individuals and also how established they are as a group, varying between degrees of collaborative or supportive styles.

Your style of leadership is a mixture of your innate personality and preferences and your learned behavior over the years. You may have been influenced by role models in your early career and have emulated the style of leadership that you appreciated as a follower. You may have been through formal leadership development programs over the years, in business school or through executive education. You may have a coach who helps you to keep your leadership style in focus and to continually improve.

Headlines from current thinking are that effective leaders:

- Have behavioral flexibility and so can adapt their style to meet the needs of the specific situation without losing authenticity (Yukl & Mahsud, 2010)
- Create psychological safety for the team to contribute (Delizonna, 2017)
- Recognize that they are incomplete and that success comes from a complete team, not an heroic individual (Ancona, Malone, Orlikowski, & Senge, 2007)

Although there may be parts of the decision-making process in which you choose to use a directive style, it's always important to follow Stephen Covey's advice: "Seek first to understand, then to be understood" (Covey,

2020). The worst thing you can do as a leader is to anchor the group to your perceptions, preferences, and opinions too early.

4.2.6 Organizational Culture

Culture has the potential to influence any of the other characteristics above. Understanding the prevailing culture helps in predicting likely behaviors.

Perhaps the most enduring description of organizational culture is, "The way things are done around here." Culture captures the unwritten rules that influence individual and group attitude and behaviors. In turn, repeated performances of attitudes and behaviors reinforces culture.

We can illustrate this in a simple A-B-C Model, as shown in Figure 4.2. The key feature of this model is that it is cyclic. Underlying attitudes shape the behavior of individuals and groups, and repeated behavior forms culture. But culture also influences current and future attitudes and behavior.

These cyclic interdependencies between attitudes, behaviors, and culture allow the development of self-reinforcing feedback loops. On the one hand, these can create a vicious cycle, in which poor attitudes lead to inappropriate behaviors and build a negative culture, which in turn

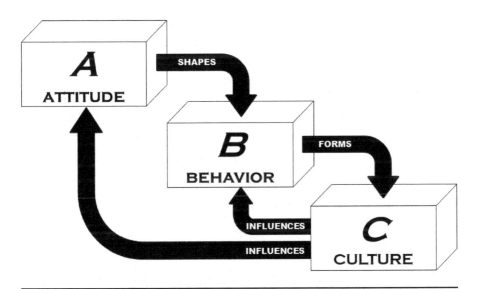

Figure 4.2 A-B-C Model of Culture (*Source:* Reproduced from Hillson [2013], used with permission)

reinforces bad attitudes and behavior. On the other, the loop can act as a virtuous cycle, with good attitudes producing appropriate behaviors and a positive culture, which acts to strengthen right attitudes and encourage good behaviors.

The saying, "Culture eats strategy for breakfast" (The Management Centre, 2020), expresses the enduring and pervasive nature of culture in influencing organizational performance in all areas.

Risk culture is an aspect of organizational culture that is directly relevant to making risky and important decisions. We explore how you as a leader can influence risk culture in Chapter 6.

4.2.7 Interacting Influences

We've seen that a number of influences affect the ability of a decision-making group to function well, including propinquity, power, group dynamics, team maturity, leadership style, and organizational culture. These each affect each other and together influence the way that risk is perceived by the group, as illustrated by Figure 4.3.

Our earlier work (Murray-Webster & Hillson, 2008) showed that these factors are not equally influential. In particular, we found that power and propinquity levels had the greatest influence on how risky and important

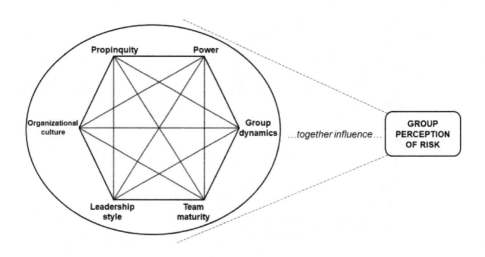

Figure 4.3   Multiple Influences on Group Risk Perception

decisions were made. The most important influence on any group decision was the individual risk attitudes of those group members with the highest perceived levels of power. The influence of power was heightened where that individual also had high propinquity, meaning that they cared a lot about the decision. If you as leader have high levels of both power and propinquity in a risky and important situation, this can result in the decision-making group just "following the leader," and as more members of the group declare for your position, the safety-in-numbers effect amplifies the view that we all agree. You may as well have made the decision on your own!

4.2.8 Summary Points on Functioning Groups

As a leader, you cannot always choose your core team, but you will have some choice in bringing in others to augment the core team to create a functioning decision-making group for a risky and important decision. One part of your work in establishing a functioning group is to select people who have appropriate competencies to add value, including diversity of experience and viewpoint. The other part is to act in a way that prevents the group from falling into the traps of either blindly following the leader or adopting a safety-in-numbers mindset.

The nature of subconscious heuristics and cognitive biases is that, even when you know that they influence you without you being consciously aware, such knowledge doesn't make them go away. Your challenge is to determine what you need to do to enable a diverse group of people to make their contribution "without fear or favor" and to ensure that differences are used to create value.

4.3 Key Points

The main learning points in this chapter include the following:

1. People make risky and important decisions, so you need to have competent individuals and a functioning group in order to make a good decision.
2. Individual competence is made up from the five PEAKS elements: personal characteristics, experience, attitudes, knowledge, and

skills. Competent decision making requires a distinct set of attributes within each of these five elements.

3. Functioning groups need to take account of factors that can otherwise skew rational decision making, including propinquity, power, group dynamics, team maturity, leadership style, and organizational culture.

4. As leader, you may need to work with individuals in your team who have limited competence, and some aspects of group behavior may also need your attention.

4.4 Looking Forward

In the next two chapters, we'll suggest ways of dealing with the complexities of individual and group perceptions and attitudes that can derail your ability to make a Risk-Intelligent Decision. Chapter 5 provides a framework to guide you. Chapter 6 then focuses on what you can do to build an effective culture for risk-based decision making: a culture that supports the implementation of the good practice shared.

References

Ancona, D., Malone, T. W., Orlikowski, W. J., and Senge, P. M. (2007). In praise of the incomplete leader. *Harvard Business Review*. February.

Covey, S. R. (2020). *The 7 Habits of Highly Effective People*, 30th anniversary edition. New York: Simon and Schuster.

Cross, J. (2013). The 11 Cs model of corporate governance. *Boardroom Dynamics*. London, UK: ICSA Publishing Ltd.

Delizonna, L. (2017). High-performing teams need psychological safety. Here's how to create it. *Harvard Business Review*. August.

French, J., and Raven, B. (1960). The bases for social power. In D. Cartwright and A. Zander (Eds.). *Group Dynamics: Research and Theory*. New York: Harper & Row.

Hillson, D. A. (2013). The A-B-C of risk culture: How to be risk-mature. *Proceedings of PMI Global Congress North America 2013,* New Orleans, LA. October 2013.

Hillson, D. A. (2015). Risk facilitation made easy. *Proceedings of PMI Global Congress Europe 2015,* London, UK. June 2002.

Janis, I. L. (1972). *Victims of groupthink: A psychological study of foreign policy decisions and fiascoes.* Boston, MA: Houghton Mifflin.

Murray-Webster, R., and Hillson, D. A. (2002). Scaling the PEAKS of project management competency. *Proceedings of PMI Europe Congress 2002,* Cannes, France. June 2002.

Murray-Webster, R., and Hillson, D. A. (2008). *Managing Group Risk Attitude.* Aldershot, UK: Gower Publishing.

The Management Centre. (2020). "Culture eats strategy for breakfast." The Management Centre. [online] Available at https://www.managementcentre. co.uk/management-consultancy/culture-eats-strategy-for-breakfast/. Accessed December 3, 2020.

The Quotations Page. (2020). The Quotations Page: Quote from William Wrigley, Jr. [online] Available at http://www.quotationspage.com/quote/29888.html. Accessed December 3, 2020.

Tuckman, B. W. (1965). Developmental sequence in small groups. *Psychological Bulletin,* 63.

Tuckman, B. W., and Jensen, M. A. C. (1977). Stages of small group development revisited. *Group and Organization Studies,* 2(4), 419–427.

Yukl, G., and Mahsud, R. (2010). Why flexible and adaptive leadership is essential. *Consulting Psychology Journal Practice and Research,* 62(2), 81–93.

Chapter 5

Intentional Choices

In Chapter 2 we built a model for making risky and important decisions. This started with an intuitive gut-feel about what might be the right decision option, without taking any conscious account of risk, and we called that a Risk-Blind Decision (Figure 2.1). We saw that you could improve that decision process by thinking about how much risk you were prepared to take in order to achieve your decision objectives. You could make a Risk-Informed Decision by understanding your risk appetite, expressing it in measurable risk thresholds, and then choosing a decision option that lay within those thresholds (Figure 2.2). This still left you driven by an intuitive internal view of how much was too much risk, which could lead you to choose an inappropriate decision option. You might also find that no option lay within your risk thresholds, or that all options would breach the overall risk capacity of your organization. The final Risk-Intelligent Decision model in Chapter 2 introduced a control loop, allowing you to choose to modify the risk thresholds you were applying to your decision by intentionally changing your risk attitude (Figure 2.4).

The Risk-Intelligent Decision model has two key drivers: your *perception* of the riskiness of the decision, and the *people* involved in making your decision. We addressed *risk perception* in Chapter 3, showing how it's influenced by a wide range of factors, including conscious, subconscious, and affective factors (the "triple strand" of influences, Figure 3.1). These factors can lead individuals and groups to make decisions that are biased and suboptimal. In Chapter 4 we looked at the *people side* of making risky and important decisions, exploring what we mean by competent individuals and functioning teams.

Throughout the past three chapters, we've highlighted areas in which you might need to make intentional changes to the way you approach your decision making in order to end up with a good decision. These include the following:

- It's important that *risk thresholds stay within organizational risk capacity*, so if your initial thresholds don't do that, you may need to *choose a different risk attitude* which allows you to modify them.
- You need to *become aware of subconscious heuristics and cognitive biases* that influence your tendency to take risk, both as an individual and in groups, and you may need to *take action to correct for any bias* that's influencing you or others.
- You need to *understand your emotional state and the way others in the group are feeling*, as these affective factors will drive your approach to risk taking and decision making. You may also need to *take steps to modify your own feelings and help others to do so*, so that you can take a more rational and considered decision.

But how do you change risk attitude? What steps can you take to understand heuristics and correct for cognitive biases or to moderate emotions in yourself and others? This chapter describes a simple framework for making these adjustments when they're necessary.

5.1 Practicing Behavioral Literacy

You may have noticed a problem with the list of changes you might need to make when you're dealing with risky and important decisions. All of the things you need to change are internal, hidden inside you and others. You can't see your attitudes, heuristics, biases, or emotions. This makes them hard to measure or modify.

Fortunately, there's a way to understand and manage things within yourself and others that you can't see, based on *emotional intelligence*. Everyone's heard of emotional intelligence, and it's become a standard item on the list of must-have characteristics for leaders of all kinds (Goleman, 1998, 2001). Some people prefer the term *emotional literacy*, which describes how well you can use the emotional intelligence that you have (Steiner & Perry, 2000). Everyone has a degree of emotional intelligence, but using it is a different matter. There are many approaches to emotional literacy which aim to help you recognize and understand your emotions, express them appropriately, and then handle them. But despite the popularity and universality of emotional intelligence or emotional literacy, not everyone is sure what they are, whether they've got them, or how to use them.

Emotional literacy is designed specifically with emotions in mind, but the approach can be applied more broadly to help you understand and manage other aspects of your internal life, including attitudes, heuristics, and biases. In our previous work (Murray-Webster & Hillson, 2008), we've modified and extended standard emotional literacy and combined it with transactional analysis and research on the triune brain to develop a simple *behavioral literacy* framework that will help you in the challenge of making risky and important decisions. We call this the *Seven As Framework*.

5.2 The Seven As Framework for Behavioral Literacy

The Seven As Framework is a simple structured process that allows you to modify the behaviors of yourself and others in an intentional and deliberate way in order to optimize the chances of achieving a desired outcome. It involves the following steps (see Figure 5.1):

- **Awareness**: What's going on?
- **Appreciation:** Why is that happening?
- **Assessment:** Is it OK?
- **Acceptance:** If it's OK, then let's carry on.
- **Assertion:** If it's not OK, then something needs to change.
- **Action:** Let's change these things.
- **Appraisal:** Is this still relevant?

Taken together, these steps provide a simple but powerful approach to understanding the hidden influences in risky decision making, allowing

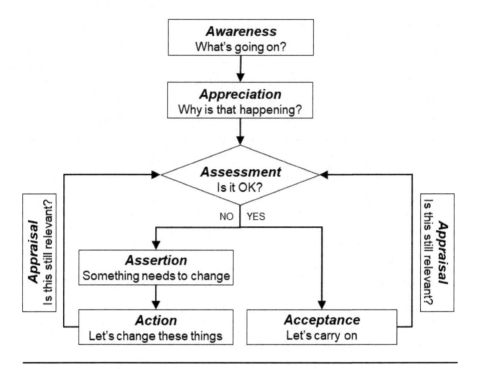

Figure 5.1 The Seven As Framework (*Source:* Adapted from Murray-Webster & Hillson [2008], used with permission)

you to make necessary changes intentionally in order to support more appropriate behavior.

You can apply the Seven As Framework to help you address your own internal environment, which gives you a powerful way to self-moderate and self-manage in the decision-making setting. But you can also use it as a leader or facilitator to help others in your decision-making group. Each of the seven steps is described in more detail below.

5.2.1 Awareness

The first step in tackling hidden influences is to understand what's going on. It's important for you to gain self-awareness of what might be affecting your own decision making, but you also need to become aware of what's happening with others in your team. Remember, you're seeking to discover three things:

- Current risk attitude
- Active heuristics and cognitive biases
- Strong emotions and feelings

Self-awareness can come through a number of routes, including:

- Reflection, self-examination, constructive introspection, or meditation
- Input from a coach, mentor, trusted friend, or colleague
- Use of structured diagnostic tools such as psychometric questionnaires
- Formal feedback, including 360° appraisal
- Behavior-based appreciative inquiry (Appreciative Inquiry Commons, 2020)

The goal is to consider your own outward behavior and discover clues that reveal your current risk attitude as well as the presence of heuristics, sources of bias, or strong emotions. Once you know these things are present, you can explore where they came from.

You can use similar discovery techniques as a leader to develop Awareness of the underlying risk attitudes of your team members, as well as biases or emotions that might be influencing their judgment in the decision-making process. Information to support development of empathy can come from the following sources:

- Observation of behaviors and conversation
- Background context from situations outside the work environment
- Cultural sensitivity, including the prevailing organizational culture
- Previous history or track record of making similar decisions

When seeking Awareness of the *current risk attitude* held by yourself or others, it might help to compare the observed risk-taking behavior with the three main risk attitudes summarized in Table 5.1 (which reproduces Table 2.1).

As you look for evidence of *sources of bias or emotion*, refer to Table 5.2 (based on Table 3.1) for a list of possible influences. You can also look back at the descriptions of each of these factors in Chapter 3 for more detail of how they operate, allowing you to spot which (if any) are having an effect on you or your colleagues in the current decision-making situation.

Table 5.1 Definition of Basic Risk Attitudes

Risk Attitude	Definition
Risk averse	Uncomfortable with uncertainty, desire to avoid or reduce threats and exploit opportunities to remove uncertainty. Would be unhappy with an uncertain outcome.
Risk tolerant	Tolerant of uncertainty, no strong desire to respond to threats or opportunities in any way. Could tolerate an uncertain outcome if necessary.
Risk seeking	Comfortable with uncertainty, no desire to avoid or reduce threats or to exploit opportunities to remove uncertainty. Would be happy with an uncertain outcome.

Source: Adapted from Murray-Webster & Hillson [2008], used with permission.

Table 5.2 Examples of Subconscious and
Affective Triple-Strand Influences

Subconscious Factors		Affective Factors
Heuristics	Cognitive Biases	
Representativeness	Propinquity	Fear
Availability	Illusion of control	Desire
Confirmation trap	Illusion of knowledge	Love
Anchoring	Intelligence trap	Hatred
Groupthink	Optimism bias	Joy
Cultural conformity	Precautionary principle	Sadness
Risky/cautious shift	Loss aversion	Anger
Follow the leader		Shame
Lure of choice		

5.2.2 Appreciation

Building on Awareness, the next step is Appreciation. Where Awareness asks "What?," Appreciation wonders "Why?" This question needs to be answered for each of the hidden influences that can affect risky decision making: risk attitude, heuristics, cognitive biases, and emotions.

Once you know the *current risk attitude* of yourself and others in your team, you can begin to explore whether or not this is appropriate. A key factor here is to know why you're holding this particular risk attitude. Is it a rational choice that you've made because you believe it leads to the right type of decision-making behavior? Or has your risk attitude been influenced by underlying influences that may have produced something inappropriate? We saw in Chapter 3 that risk attitude is driven by your perception of risk, and this in turn is influenced by the triple stand of conscious, subconscious, and affective factors.

When you're aware of the operation of heuristics, the presence of sources of bias, or the existence of strong influential emotions, it's important to know why they have arisen, so that they can be addressed and modified if necessary.

Your brain has developed each of the *heuristics* in Table 5.2 in order to simplify the task of making sense of complex situations by drawing on previous experience and creating simple "rules of thumb." Each heuristic provides a shortcut that says, "When you see something like this, it probably means that." Because heuristics operate in a consistent manner, always producing the same type of influence, they are relatively easy to spot.

For example, if you immediately assume that one of your decision options has a certain set of characteristics, ask yourself why you're making this assumption. If the answer is "Because I've seen this before," then you may be subject to the representativeness heuristic. If you say, "I knew it was going to be like this, and I was right," there's probably a confirmation trap in operation. "I suspect everyone thinks the same" indicates groupthink, and, "The boss told me it would be like this" suggests you're following the leader.

In the same way, *cognitive biases* affect your judgment in a systematic way, and it's relatively easy to test for their presence by asking focused questions. For example, by asking, "Is this decision particularly important to me or anyone else?," you can check for propinquity. "Does anyone have particular insights into this situation?" may reveal that someone has the illusion of knowledge or is caught in the intelligence trap.

It can sometimes be difficult to understand the root causes of *strong emotions,* but it's important to try. Knowing why you or another person is feeling something allows you to examine whether it's proportionate and appropriate, or whether it's an overreaction or an irrelevance. Sometimes strong emotions are driven by misunderstanding or misinterpretation or by invalid assumptions. At other times they can result from trigger events that release memories of past experiences in which strong emotions previously occurred, tricking the brain into repeating those same emotions as if they were real in the current situation.

The challenge when seeking to appreciate the underlying reasons and causes for these hidden influences is that you're always working remotely at arm's length. It's rarely possible to know with absolute certainty why these factors are at work in a person, even when you're looking within yourself. Interpretation is based on observed behaviors and knowledge of past history, both of which are likely to be partial and incomplete. Appreciation requires you to try to recognize and understand what's going on and respect it even if you don't agree. Although both Awareness and Appreciation are based on observations and assessments that are partial and subjective, nevertheless, taken together, they provide a firm foundation for the subsequent steps in the Seven As Framework, allowing you to test the effect of these influences and make intentional changes where necessary.

5.2.3 Assessment

Once you've made your best evaluation of what's going on and why, it's time to consider whether things are OK or not, given the characteristics of the risky and important decision. The Assessment step involves taking what you now understand about yourself and the others in your decision-making group, and determining whether it is likely to help or hinder you in making a good decision.

Essentially this is a predictive step, asking "What if?" Imagine that you and your colleagues retained your current risk attitudes; would that enable appropriate risk-taking behavior that allows you to choose clearly between the decision options? Or might they result in your taking too much or too little risk, prejudicing your ability to meet your decision objectives?

In the same way, consider active heuristics or cognitive biases—are they leading you toward or away from an unbiased decision process? Where biases are evident, is their influence constructive or distracting?

As for the emotions that you and others are currently feeling, are these likely to get in the way of an open and considered discussion of the decision options, or might they cause inter- or intra-personal tensions that could color the judgment of individuals or the group?

It's quite possible that for each of these considerations, the answer could be positive. Yes, our existing risk attitudes align with the amount of risk-taking needed to stay within risk thresholds and risk capacity, and they allow us to choose a suitable decision option that meets our objectives. No, none of the active heuristics or cognitive biases are a cause for concern. And no, any emotions currently in play probably won't affect our ability to work together as a team to make a good decision.

Alternatively, you might identify at least one problem area among the wide range of potential hidden influences.

At this point, the Seven As Framework offers two paths, depending on whether the answer to the Assessment question, "Is it OK?" is Yes or No. If the current situation is OK, then we can move to Acceptance; otherwise we need to choose Assertion and Action.

5.2.4 Acceptance

Where Assessment indicates that there is no cause for concern, the Seven As Framework includes an Acceptance step, moving forward to make a Risk-Intelligent Decision without further intervention. But this is much more than a simple "do nothing." Acceptance is a positive recognition that an explicit and considered examination of potential hidden influences has not revealed anything that requires active change.

This good news deserves marking in some way. In the rare cases in which you're making a risky and important decision alone, you might indulge in a metaphorical pat on the back as a mark of self-affirmation that all is well. But where you're working with colleagues in a decision-making group, it would be helpful for you as leader to positively state that together you're good to go. This doesn't need any great fanfare or ceremony, but you can explain to your team that you've taken seriously the possibility of distracting hidden influences and nothing appears to be amiss. This could offer an opportunity for you to seek input from colleagues, to check if you've missed anything. Maybe they're aware of something that you didn't see, and that you might need to go back to consider.

Regardless of whether something comes to light that you didn't consider in the Awareness, Appreciation, and Assessment steps, it's vital that Acceptance is not seen as the end of the process. Figure 5.1 includes a feedback loop from Acceptance to Assessment, marked Appraisal, discussed below.

5.2.5 Assertion

When the Assessment of the current situation indicates the need for change, someone will need to make a conscious choice to challenge the status quo, questioning the prevailing mode of thinking. This role often falls to the leader. The task is easier when you're making a decision alone, but even then, there's a need for intentional intervention, self-modification, and self-management. The Assertion step in the Seven As Framework is where such challenge takes place, either for groups or for yourself.

Some might think that this step is simple. The prior steps have revealed what's going on and why and indicated the need for a change of behavior. All that's needed now is for the leader to state what's required, and it will happen. While this might work in a few instances, particularly when the decision-making group is well established and mature, more often the Assertion step needs careful attention.

Challenging interventions are easier to describe than to do. They always go against the natural flow of the way people think or feel, requiring you and others to move away from instinctive gut-feel preferences. The following skills will help you as leader to Assert the need for change in a way that creates commitment to action:

- *Assertiveness.* It's self-evident that the Assertion step involves assertiveness. But this requires a high degree of personal courage and resilience from the leader, demonstrating the ability to be assertive without being aggressive or manipulative. While emphasizing the need to moderate the current direction of travel, the leader must balance self-assurance and confidence with humility, being firm and direct without threatening or denigrating others.
- *Goal focus.* Always emphasize the end point. Why is this decision risky and important? What decision objectives are we aiming to achieve and why do they matter? What are the implications of a suboptimal decision? When you and your team are convinced of the importance of making a good decision, persuasion to change will be easier.
- *Framing.* Use of appropriate language is vital. The need for change must be expressed in terms that create common ground among the team, without personal criticism. Inclusive language is helpful, presenting potential changes as helpful alternatives toward a shared goal.
- *Constructive discontent.* It's important to engage with individuals who hold different views, using their sense of unease with the current situation to create energy toward change. Encourage free expression of differing positions and opinions before working toward group consensus. The challenge here is to turn discontent and criticism into positive motivation toward action, which requires

effective interpersonal skills from the leader, making allies of critics and turning detractors into advocates for change.

- *Conflict handling.* You can't please all of the people all of the time. Despite your skillful use of the techniques listed above, it's almost inevitable that some dissenters will remain unconvinced. This is where your conflict resolution skills come into play. There are many approaches to conflict handling, each of which is suitable for different settings. The effective leader will have several such tools available, with the ability to select the most appropriate in order to resolve conflict in a context of mutual respect and trust.

The outcome from Assertion is two-fold: recognition that change is necessary and a commitment to take action. This leads naturally to the next step in the Seven As Framework.

5.2.6 Action

If Assertion is the point of intentional choice, then Action is the point at which we implement that choice and actually do something. Up to this point the Seven As Framework has only involved analysis, but the process is a waste of time if analysis isn't turned into action.

Earlier in this book, we identified "commitment to action" as a vital component of a good decision-making process. Primarily, this refers to a commitment by yourself and your decision-making team to follow through on the decision option that you select and actually put it into practice. But "commitment to action" is a general characteristic of effective leadership which is relevant in multiple ways. And this point in the Seven As Framework is no exception.

If you've gone through the earlier steps of the framework, becoming Aware of what's going on and Appreciating why, Assessing its suitability toward meeting your objectives and deciding that it's not OK, and then Asserting the need for change, it's vital then to follow through with a commitment to take Action. That's why this A is an essential part of the Seven As Framework.

As always, action planning is essential. The SMART acronym provides a good reminder that actions must be clearly defined to be Specific, Measurable, Achievable, Relevant, and Timely. They must be agreed, accepted, and owned by a named individual who takes accountability for their completion. And outcomes need to be reviewed to discover whether these actions actually result in a changed risk attitude, or behavior that is less influenced by heuristics and cognitive biases, or an understanding and management of prevailing emotions. In Chapter 7 we'll explore some of the actions that are effective in changing risk attitude, challenging and correcting for heuristics and cognitive biases, or moderating strong emotion.

5.2.7 Appraisal

Figure 5.1 shows that the Seven As Framework doesn't end with either Acceptance or Action. After each of these steps, there's a loop back to reconsider whether anything has changed that might require a different choice. We call this Appraisal, when you check whether the path you're currently following is still relevant.

Your initial Assessment of the various hidden influences may have concluded that nothing required active management at this stage, leading you to Acceptance. Or you may have recognized the need to modify your behavior through Assertion and Action. But things change, especially in situations that are risky and important. There may be significant movement in the decision context. Characteristics of one of the decision options might change, making it more or less risky or desirable. The personal circumstances of someone in the team may cause emotional upheaval or a change in their attitude to risk.

For any of these reasons, a situation that you could previously Accept may now need more active intervention. Conversely, where you've taken Action to adopt a different risk attitude, to counter unhelpful heuristics or cognitive biases, or to address strong emotions, your Action might have been sufficiently successful for you to be able to continue without further change.

Appraisal is a reminder to check back periodically to see what's changed in the hidden landscape of attitudes, subconscious influences and emotions. The Appraisal feedback loops shown in Figure 5.1 go back to Assessment, asking whether the situation is still OK. Maybe you'd decided to Accept the status quo, but is that still the right thing to do? Or after Asserting the need for change and taking Action, perhaps you can now Accept the new situation?

Including Appraisal within the Seven As Framework ensures that you maintain the optimal environment for making risky and important decisions throughout the decision-making process.

5.3 When to Use the Seven As Framework

The Seven As Framework provides a powerful way to understand and manage influences that would otherwise remain hidden and uncontrolled. This framework has a particular role in the context of making risky and important decisions. We've seen how the Risk-Intelligent Decision includes a control loop allowing you to moderate risk thresholds by choosing a different risk attitude (Figure 2.4), and the Seven As Framework provides the mechanism for making that choice.

As a reflexive leader, you'll know that self-awareness and self-management always comes before tackling others, and we recommend that you practice self-examination regularly, especially before making a decision. You should develop the ability to rapidly diagnose your current risk attitude, test its appropriateness for the situation at hand, and self-moderate as necessary.

But you'll also need to be able to lead others in your decision-making team on the same journey, following the simple steps in the Seven As Framework and helping the group to adopt a shared risk attitude that enables you to make good decisions together.

5.4 Key Points

In this chapter, we've discovered the following:

1. To make a good risky and important decision, you may need to address or modify several invisible and inherent factors, including changing risk attitude, correcting for sources of bias, or moderating emotions and feelings.
2. Behavioral literacy provides a way to understand and manage hidden influences.
3. The Seven As Framework offers a structured approach to behavioral literacy, starting with Awareness, Appreciation, and Assessment.

This may lead to Acceptance of the status quo, or Assertion and Action may be needed. Either way, the framework includes Appraisal, to check whether anything significant has changed.

4. You should practice behavioral literacy for yourself first, before leading others toward improved understanding and management of their own internal drivers.

5.5 Looking Forward

In Chapter 6, we switch our focus to culture to explore how you as a leader can create and sustain the risk culture needed to make intentional choices and Risk-Intelligent Decisions.

References

Appreciative Inquiry Commons. (2020). https://appreciativeinquiry.champlain .edu/

Goleman, D. (1998). *Working with Emotional Intelligence*. London, UK: Bloomsbury Publishing.

Goleman, D. (2001). *Emotionally Intelligent Workplace: How to Select for, Measure and Improve Emotional Intelligence in Individuals, Groups and Organizations*. Hackensack, NJ: Jossey-Bass.

Murray-Webster, R., and Hillson, D. A. (2008). *Managing Group Risk Attitude*. Aldershot, UK: Gower Publishing.

Steiner, C., and Perry, P. (2000). *Achieving Emotional Literacy*, 2nd edition. Lyndhurst, NJ: Barnes & Noble.

Chapter 6

Shaping Risk Culture

This chapter provides the final piece in the puzzle of how to make consistently good decisions in all risky and important situations—arguably the most vital part of your role as a leader.

In Chapters 1 and 2, we explored what makes a good decision, and we suggested that Risk-Intelligent Decisions take account of both the decision information (objectives, context, and options) and the decision makers (individual risk preferences, group risk culture, and commitment to action). They also reflect a way forward that adopts an intentionally chosen attitude to risk and a set of risk thresholds that reflect the risk appetite and capacity to take risk at that time.

This sounds easy, but we know that there are many hidden influences on our perception of what's true, what isn't, what might happen, how likely those situations are, and whether they would be good or bad for our objectives. Perception is reality for individuals and decision-making groups, and in Chapters 3 and 4, we argued that for you to make good decisions in risky and important situations, you need to understand what influences perception, as well as having ways of judging whether people are competent and whether decision-making groups are fit for purpose.

In Chapter 5 we introduced the Seven As Framework. This outlines the process needed to intentionally modify risk attitude, ensuring that the perceptions of decision makers are understood and that the group corrects for the biasing effect of heuristics, cognitive biases, and emotions. This assumes, of course, that the group has brought all the foreseeable data to the decision-making table in the first place—those facts now that are pertinent and the uncertainties that would matter to the decision objectives should they occur. All this is important to ensure that the decision makers do not "sleepwalk" into a suboptimal decision.

To lead your organization so that it consistently makes good decisions in risky and important situations, there are two more things for you to consider.

Firstly, how do you set an example that ensures that decision information is as complete as necessary to carry the "weight" of the decision? When the decision really matters, you really don't want to overlook anything obvious. How do you:

- Ensure that people are bringing the risks they perceive forward for discussion and not discounting them for some reason?
- Make it safe for people to share ideas and perspectives, however "out there" they may seem?

Secondly, when the decision information is as complete as possible, how do you create the conditions so that the Seven As Framework, which is simple in theory, can work in practice? How will you create and nurture a culture for risky and important decision making that:

- Provides the environment for people to develop Awareness and Appreciation of self and others?
- Supports the time taken to Assess situations so people know when and where to be Assertive and Act to challenge the prevailing attitudes?
- Accepts when a situation is good enough to move forward and provides ongoing Appraisal?

The answers to these questions come from an exploration of organizational culture, and an aspect of this that has been shown to be vital for risk management and risky decision making to be effective: risk culture.

6.1 Organizational Culture

Many leading scholars (e.g., Schein, 1985; Johnson & Scholes, 1992; Brown, 1995) have described the factors that influence culture and declare that it is the most difficult thing to change in an organization. Although some aspects of culture are visible (dress codes, mission statements, processes and procedures, communication style, etc.), many other aspects of culture are either hidden from view (values, traditions, power structures beyond the organization chart, etc.), or deeply nuanced (rituals, stories, etc.).

Long histories are not the easiest organizational attribute for a leader to inherit. With deeply embedded ways of working can come long memories and stories of the last person who tried to do things differently. As organizational agility and flexibility become increasingly valued capabilities, there is a growing interest in how to build a culture that is exploratory, innovative, and adaptive, yet that's still able to uphold standards and conduct and that also gets the most out of past investments in products and services.

Changing overall organizational culture is beyond our scope here, but a subset of organizational culture is relevant to making risky and important decisions—namely, the organization's risk culture. What is your role as a leader in shaping and upholding this?

6.2 Risk Culture

In 2012, the Institute of Risk Management conducted research and published guidance on risk culture. In that work they defined risk culture as *"the values, beliefs, knowledge and understanding about risk shared by a group of people with a common purpose"* (Institute of Risk Management, 2012).

Why is risk culture important? Is it equally or more important than other aspects of organizational culture, such as people, safety, sustainability?

Risk culture is important because, as explained in Chapter 1, in the UK, the governance codes for listed companies and charities all require leaders to pay express attention to upholding a culture for risk taking that supports strategy. Boards are required to ensure that strategic plans protect existing value and create new value (Financial Reporting Council, 2014; The Charity Commission, 2017).

Setting and upholding a risk culture is not trivial. Although the board is accountable, the executive leaders of the organization have the day-to-day, decision-to-decision responsibility for creating a culture in which attitudes and behaviors support good decision making.

In Figure 4.2, we introduced the A-B-C Model that highlights the relationship between attitudes, behaviors, and culture, showing how these three variables influence each other to create a self-sustaining environment for organizational life, including decision making. There are two types of behavior that form the point of control. The first is our own patterns of daily behavior, and the second is the behaviors we encourage in others. We cannot "see" underlying attitudes, but these are communicated loudly and clearly through our behaviors, which in turn shape and sustain the culture.

So, how will you build a coherent and cohesive risk culture—that is, one in which there is alignment and consistency between intended behaviors (in principle) and what actually happens (in practice)? There is no option but to decide how you will behave in a few key areas and then to be visibly consistent.

As you lead your team toward informed choices and risk-intelligent decision making, you'll need to address four aspects of behavior that are essential for shaping a mature risk culture:

- How you communicate
- How you enable information sharing
- How you support people
- How you recognize and reward risk taking

Each of these behaviors contributes to creating and supporting a mature risk culture.

6.2.1 How You Communicate

How do you communicate clearly your expectations about managing risk within defined risk thresholds, reducing threats and exploiting opportunities to the levels that fit the appetite and capacity? What you say and do—and what you don't say and don't do—all have equal influence in communicating your intentions and commitment.

Leaders carry a great responsibility, some might argue a burden, to "walk the walk and talk the talk." This is often called "tone from the top," but it is much more. You also need to ensure that clarity of communication about tolerable levels of risk is continually reinforced and that you seek out feedback about how you're doing, adapting as necessary based on that feedback.

Many leaders have found ways of doing this successfully when it comes to safety risk or conduct risk. Perhaps this is because it's relatively simple to state that your safety risk threshold is zero accidents, or where conduct risk aims at zero reportable incidents. It is more challenging in other risky areas where the tolerance for risk is something other than zero.

The situation also gets more complicated when you are under pressure. It is normal for people to have less conscious control of their behaviors when things are not going to plan, as the control mechanisms we have when things are calm become overridden by inherent preferences and subconscious habits and emotions. So, under pressure, your challenge is to make sure there is no observable gap between the intended values and behaviors and what you actually say and do when there is bad news or when there are commercial or operational crises.

Many leaders embrace challenge and feedback. Others find it more difficult. Making good decisions in risky and important situations relies on curiosity, diversity of thought, and the ability to challenge strongly held positions. How you behave when people speak out through formal channels or as part of team discussions will also shape culture. A mature risk culture is one in which challenge is expected and sought by everyone and where ideas that are dismissed are done so respectfully. That starts with you.

6.2.2 How You Enable Information Sharing

To support a culture in which challenge is respectfully provided and graciously heard, two other aspects of risk culture are relevant to the effectiveness of information flow: empowerment and transparency.

How do you ensure that your team feels empowered to identify risks and to manage risks in line with defined controls—or to suggest how controls could be improved?

Conversations about risk are never "true." As a future construct, risks are a feature of our perceptions, and so everyone's view is worth hearing. That view may not be shared by others, and it may not withstand robust challenge, but if a person's point of view is summarily dismissed, either verbally or non-verbally, they won't feel empowered to speak up next time. You have probably been party to conversations about risks that were dismissed as ridiculous, yet the risks happened and the organization wasn't prepared.

Fortunately, empowerment can be built into the culture. You do it by demonstrating that you trust others, helping them to learn from experiences, and ensuring that they can save face if they've made a mistake. You also need to make it clear that you won't tolerate people belittling others or being scornful about their ideas and perceptions about risks. You can respond to whistleblowing with a genuine intention to learn, rather than being defensive. These practical behaviors demonstrate the extent to which you're prepared to empower your team to take responsibility for their actions, confident in your support and trust.

Transparency about available information, insights, and learning helps to build a culture of trust that supports empowerment. Clearly, there are constraints about disclosure of some information because it's commercially sensitive or because sharing it would contravene data protection legislation. Your role is to make clear where the boundaries lie and then stick to them. Cultures that tolerate gossip and disclosure of personal information do not encourage others to be transparent. They can create a context in which it is too risky to share personal views about risks. Your organization will be the worse if this happens.

You can also encourage transparency by overtly ensuring that there is learning from actual problems/issues/variances from plans. All too often, unwanted results are hidden because the prevailing culture blames others rather than encouraging learning. This isn't to say that people should not be held accountable for their area of influence, but variances from plan are rarely one person's fault. High-performing teams take collective responsibility for learning. This is invaluable in learning about issues that have occurred and if/how these were predicted and managed.

6.2.3 How You Support People

Understanding and managing risk and risky decision making is not simple. Predicting the future is never easy, and there are many concepts and ideas to understand, as we've seen in earlier chapters.

Role-specific learning and development for all staff is vital to enable them to:

- Understand risk as a perception-based, future-looking construct
- Identify risks in their area and describe them clearly

- Know what they are empowered to do
- Communicate and challenge appropriately

Often in organizations, risk specialists are employed to take the load away from leaders and to come up with a feasible set of risk information that can withstand scrutiny by the relevant governance boards. Often this information reflects the risk preferences and perspectives of the risk specialist, not the leaders in the organization. Detailed, specialist risk analysis methods don't need to be understood by everyone, but a mature risk culture doesn't have risk work done by risk specialists in isolation. Rather it supports staff to take part in risk-based conversations with confidence. The most valuable skills of risk specialists in building an effective risk culture are facilitation and appropriate challenge. These skills hold leaders to account and ensure that alternative perspectives are explored and decisions are de-biased. One of the most important things you can do as a leader is to hire a suitably experienced and skilled risk facilitator who understands all the relevant concepts and ideas and who has the gravitas and confidence to challenge upwards and sustain an environment in which decision makers can have a robust conversation and make good choices. This is not a junior position—the right person will be a major asset to your organization.

6.2.4 How You Recognize and Reward Risk Taking

This final area for you to consider as you lead your team toward informed choices and risk-intelligent decision making is in some ways the most difficult. How do you recognize and reward informed risk taking?

At one level that might sound easy: you recognize and reward performance against agreed goals and targets. But therein lies the challenge. As discussed in Chapter 1, a good decision is not the same as a planned outcome. Sometimes people are lucky: they make a bad decision but get away with it because other things change to recover the situation. Sometimes people are unlucky: they make a good decision but unforeseeable conditions lead to an unwanted result.

When it comes to building risk culture, your performance management process may be rewarding the wrong behaviors. It's difficult to get right, but getting lucky shouldn't be rewarded more than a risk-informed approach. Neither should playing it safe be rewarded more than balanced "within appetite" risk taking. Recognition and reward need to be focused on informed risk taking that seeks to create and maximize value within the constraints of relevant organizational policies and standards. Most organizations we have encountered struggle in this area. You will probably need to give some thought to how this principle can be adopted within your performance management framework. You may need to influence others outside of your team to ensure that appropriate risk taking is recognized and rewarded.

Key to getting this right is to encourage people to explain and document their decision-making process in risky and important situations and for this to be agreed. This is good practice anyway and can help build a culture where good decision making is acknowledged as requiring a process and capability, not based on experience-based hunches. Then, when faced with unexpected results (either much worse or much better than plan), the information to support reward and recognition is the decision process, not the outcome.

6.3 Why Risk Culture Matters

Risk culture affects all organizational activity to identify, analyze, and respond to threats and opportunities to objectives. The culture for risk is influencing the quality of conversation and the quality of risk information in your organization now.

Risky and important decisions are influenced by the quality of decision information and the competence of decision makers. These in turn are helped or hindered by the ability of your people to understand risk, to speak about it with confidence, and to appreciate how their perceptions and those of others are being influenced and biased by a range of factors.

We're not trying to bring decision making to a stand-still by raising these important issues to be addressed. The goal is not to create a culture that fears getting things wrong or ends up with analysis paralysis. The purpose is to give you confidence that when things really matter, you have a way forward to make the best decision you can in the circumstances. And addressing risk culture will improve the quality of risk information and conversation in your organization in all circumstances.

Every small thing you do to be a role model for the attitudes and behaviors that build and sustain a mature risk culture will be worth it.

6.4 Key Points

In this chapter, we've discovered the following:

1. Risky and important decision making is significantly complex. It's vital to expose information that is complete enough to support the weight of the decision, and to shape a risk culture that can understand and modify hidden influences.
2. It is your responsibility to shape a risk culture in which attitudes and behaviors support decision making.
3. Four aspects of behavior are essential for shaping a mature risk culture: how you communicate, how you enable information sharing, how you support people, and how you recognize and reward risk taking.
4. As a leader and role model in your organization, you have a direct impact on the ability of your team to understand risk, to speak about it with confidence, and to appreciate how their perceptions and those of others might be biased.

6.5 Looking Forward

In Chapter 7, we take a look back at the book so far, anticipating some of your "Yes, but . . ." questions and challenges. We raise questions that leaders commonly ask us and provide our best advice about how to deal with them.

References

Brown, A. (1995). *Organisational Culture*, 2nd edition. London, UK: Pitman Publishing.

Financial Reporting Council. (2014). *Guidance on Risk Management, Internal Control and Related Financial and Business Reporting.* London, UK: Financial Reporting Council.

Institute of Risk Management. (2012). *Risk Culture: Resources for Practitioners.* London, UK: Institute of Risk Management.

Johnson, G., and Scholes, K. (1992). *Exploring Corporate Strategy.* London, UK: FT Prentice Hall.

Schein, E. H. (1985). *Organisational Culture and Leadership.* San Francisco, CA: Jossey Bass.

The Charity Commission. (2017). *Charity Governance Code.* London, UK: The Charity Commission.

Chapter 7

"Yes, but . . ."

What have we learned so far?

- Leaders routinely have to make decisions that matter in circumstances that are uncertain.
- To make a risky and important decision, you have to take proper account of risk, and Chapter 2 describes how to make a Risk-Intelligent Decision.
- This type of decision is based on your perception of risk, which in turn is influenced by a wide range of factors, which we explore in Chapter 3.
- Decisions are made by people, and Chapter 4 talks about how to ensure that you're working with competent individuals operating within a functioning team.
- It's a fact of life that both individuals and groups are subject to inherent biases, and you need to have a way of understanding and managing these hidden influences. We address this in Chapter 5.
- To make good decisions in risky and important situations, all these elements need to be done within the context of a culture that understands and takes account of risk. We talk about the behaviors that support and shape risk culture in Chapter 6.

Hopefully this has all made good sense to you, and it resonates well with your experience of the challenges of making risky and important decisions. But you live and work in the real world, which differs in many ways from the idealized situation described in books like this. As you've read through the preceding chapters, we expect that from time to time you'll have thought, "Yes, but . . ."!

So this chapter considers fifteen typical objections or problems (see Table 7.1) that you might encounter while putting all of this into practice, outlining some common potential pitfalls and offering ways you might overcome them.

Table 7.1 Typical "Yes, but . . ." Questions and Concerns

1	I'm too busy to spend the time required for a Risk-Intelligent Decision process, especially if I also have to run through the Seven As. Why shouldn't I just make the best possible decision now, then make any necessary course corrections later?
2	There'll always be good and bad luck involved, so surely we can just go with our best guess for now and bounce back if things turn out badly?
3	My company treats all decisions as risky and important and expects me to apply the same process to all decisions.
4	I find it difficult to know at what level to define decision objectives and how to define thresholds for these. Strategic objectives are very high level, but operational objectives seem too tactical. What advice do you have on this?
5	Defining the "change nothing" option can be a challenge when there is a big opportunity on the table and no one wants to think about not going for it. How can I best deal with this?
6	You recommend understanding and addressing the various influences on risk perception, but is it really possible to "unpick" the triple strand? Isn't the combined effect of influences too complex to separate, especially when there's a group involved?
7	I know that it's important to pay attention to weak signals—how does that fit into your approach?
8	I work for a small company, and I have to make all strategic decisions alone. How should I modify your advice?
9	My team is dysfunctional, and they don't respect my leadership. Strong characters in the team are used to getting their own way and others just roll over. They just won't accept it if I try to introduce this type of approach to decision making.
10	Everyone in my decision-making group agrees with me, or at least they say they do. Maybe I recruited people to the team in my own image, or it might be groupthink, or possibly they really do all agree with me. What should I do?
11	I'm self-aware enough to know that I'm not good at the people stuff. How then can I follow your advice?
12	My colleagues have different risk preferences from mine. How should I lead the group when we make risky and important decisions? Should I try to influence them toward my perspective?
13	Whenever we make a decision, everyone agrees, then no one does anything differently. How do I encourage commitment to action?
14	I'm working with a virtual team—how can I work out what they're thinking and feeling?
15	My team is multicultural—how should I take account of different cultural norms?

Real life is messy, and neat solutions are rarely the whole answer, but we hope you will find encouragement in what follows.

1. *I'm too busy to spend the time required for a Risk-Intelligent Decision process, especially if I also have to run through the Seven As. Why shouldn't I just make the best possible decision now, then make any necessary course corrections later?*

If you're too busy to spend appropriate time on making risky and important decisions, then you're too busy! The clue is in the name: these decisions really matter because they have a big impact on strategic or long-term operational objectives; and they involve significant uncertainty arising from the risk associated with different decision options and a complex, unstable, or changing context.

You're right that following the steps to make a Risk-Intelligent Decision takes time and effort. But consider the alternative. Deciding quickly increases the risk that you choose a suboptimal option. You may need to change course in future, which could incur additional cost and disruption (and changing course later may not even be possible in some cases). If you move forward without taking time to engage key stakeholders to gain their commitment to action, they may not give you the support you need, reducing the chances of a successful decision outcome.

The good news is that following the recommended steps in the Risk-Intelligent Decision doesn't have to take a lot of time—it's a structured way of thinking. It's possible to streamline the process without leaving out any important steps, especially when you get used to this way of making decisions. But if you're moving quickly, be sure to document your thinking when you make the decision, so that you and others can understand why you took the course you did.

You could also set aside protected time in your diary for decision making, allowing you to focus on what's risky and important without interruption or distraction. Maybe you can delegate less strategic work to colleagues in order to make space for this.

2. *There'll always be good and bad luck involved, so surely we can just go with our best guess for now and bounce back if things turn out badly?*

Well yes you could—lots of people do! It depends how much the decision matters to what's important to the organization and its stakeholders.

Sometimes the decision matters because the core values and strategy of the organization are at risk—getting it wrong would seriously destroy value. Or perhaps the consequences for your organization's reputation would be game changing if you keep changing your mind. Strategy is often described as "the pattern of decisions made by the organization." Only you will know how well you could cope financially and/or reputationally if you get it wrong.

If you do get it wrong, you might be able to bounce back, depending on the resilience of your organization. And of course, a truly resilient organization might even "bounce forward," recovering and progressing to a better situation than the previous one. But it may be unwise to assume that you can always recover if things turn out badly. Resilience needs to be planned for and thought through carefully—it doesn't just happen. Heroic leadership in a crisis tends to only have short-term effects, and it's better to work out in advance what you'll do if things go wrong.

So, when it really matters, maybe it's too risky to rely on your best guess without any further consideration. It might even be so risky that bouncing back wouldn't be possible. Our advice always starts with understanding objectives, what's at risk. If you can get consensus on this in your decision-making group then it will help you to decide how much effort it's worth putting into making sure that the attitudes chosen and decision made fits the situation.

3. *My company treats all decisions as risky and important and expects me to apply the same process to all decisions.*

While it sounds impressive to say, "All our decisions are risky and important," it's actually not true, at least not to the same degree. In Chapter 1, we described some decisions as "more equal than others" because they involve a higher level of risk and are more important. Some decisions don't have a significant impact on strategic or long-term operational objectives, but they are more tactical and immediate. Or the decision context is stable and the decision options are well defined and understood. In many cases, you have no problem gaining the commitment of people who you need to support and implement the chosen outcome. These types of decisions lie outside our definition of "risky and important." It may not be necessary or appropriate to give them the same level of attention that really risky and important decisions deserve. More simple tactical decisions still matter of course, and you need to think carefully about your decision objectives, decision context, and decision options. But they just don't demand the same degree of effort.

If you were to apply the same rigorous decision-making process to all decisions, you're likely to focus too much on smaller decisions and not enough on the really big ones. Instead, we have a couple of suggestions.

- *Push back.* Just because "the company demands" something doesn't mean it must always be so. Make the case with your colleagues and peers for a more nuanced and targeted approach to decision making. Explain the need to be "appropriate," seeking to apply the right amount of time, effort, and process to match the riskiness and importance of each decision. Emphasize the efficiency benefits of spending more time on the decisions that matter most.
- *Prioritize.* Develop a simple way to screen and rank decisions so that you can identify which ones truly are risky and important. If *all* decisions are high priority, *none* are high priority. Top-priority decisions are the most risky (with more variation in risk thresholds) and most important (affecting strategic objectives).

4. *I find it difficult to know at what level to define decision objectives and how to define thresholds for these. Strategic objectives are very high level, but operational objectives seem too tactical. What advice do you have on this?*

This is a practical problem that's very common. It's compounded when objectives are not mutually exclusive, where performance on two objectives may be complementary or in opposition.

It's worth spending some time to define objectives and thresholds at a level at which they can be understood and measured, even if this involves a few cycles of trial and error. Objectives that are difficult to measure are not very useful—how do you know when you've achieved them? Measures could be financial or non-financial, and you may need to find proxy measures that are meaningful in your context.

The best measures are leading indicators, giving you early warning that an objective may be in jeopardy. For example, if a healthcare service aims to prioritize patient outcomes, the time between referral and treatment for medical procedures is a reasonable leading indicator.

You should also pay attention to the number of decision objectives. It can become counter-productive to have more than five or six objectives for any single decision context. More than that can make the process very unwieldly. However, most risky and important decisions affect more than one or two objectives, if you consider the whole decision context. You need the smallest number of measurable objectives that span the decision context, and you need to understand the relationship between them. One proven technique for exploring this area is *quality function deployment* (Hauser & Clausing, 1988). A good facilitator would help you work through the objectives at risk, how much they matter to key stakeholders, and the relationship between those objectives. This involves determining which objectives are givens (where you'd expect the risk thresholds to be tight), which are complementary, which you could optimize at the expense of others, and which you could trade if you had to.

Because the objectives at risk are at the heart of this approach, we advise you to spend some time on this, but always on the understanding that there's no perfect solution. All measures can be manipulated; no expression of objectives will cover all bases, you just need to find the best fit for your situation.

5. *Defining the "change nothing" option can be a challenge when there is a big opportunity on the table and no one wants to think about not going for it. How can I best deal with this?*

There are two reasons why we would encourage you to make sure the "change nothing" or "do nothing differently" option is defined, even if doing this work is not immediately valued by the team.

Firstly, it's impossible to know whether you've made the best decision in the situation if you have no point of comparison. It can be easy to fall into the trap of thinking that "change nothing" means that everything stays the same—that may be faulty thinking. Perhaps the decision is being taken in the context of an eroding baseline, and if you change nothing you'll end up reducing margins or reducing staff loyalty because the competition is standing still. Sometimes, using the words on Willem de Kooning's art installation in Rotterdam, "I have to change to stay the same" (Willem de Kooning, quoted in Jack Cowart, 1979). In other situations, "change nothing" could be against an improving baseline—for example, if productivity in an operation is increasing without any further investment.

Secondly, the very act of defining the baseline can help to reframe the decision options you're considering. It's easy to fall into mental traps of only seeking information to support your preferred option or to be anchored to a solution that is not ideal. It's always worth spending time to challenge the aspects that may be irrationally skewing your judgment. Try reframing the decision in terms of opportunity cost, asking, "What value could be destroyed by pursuing this opportunity?" This may energize your team to compare the change-nothing baseline with the opportunity costs associated with a change.

Of course, some decisions will be pretty obvious to most in the decision-making group, with benefits that are so large and indisputable that you can just go for it. If you find yourself in this position, we strongly advise documenting the decision that was made, including the assumptions. This isn't about bureaucracy or (just) providing an audit trail to protect decision makers in future; it's another way of double checking the logic pre-decision and learning in the future.

6. *You recommend understanding and addressing the various influences on risk perception, but is it really possible to "unpick" the triple strand? Isn't the combined effect of influences too complex to separate, especially when there's a group involved?*

We agree it would be a futile and impossible exercise to try to understand completely all the different conscious, subconscious, and affective factors that are influencing the perceptions and risk attitude of every individual member of the decision-making group. The whole point of the triple strand is that, at the point of choosing an attitude to risk in any particular situation, people can't be sure what is driving their perception and choices, precisely because the three strands are tightly interwoven. For example, recent past experience may lead you to perceive the current situation as manageable, heightened by the availability heuristic (most recent, most memorable). If this is combined with a personal desire to press ahead because it would give you an opportunity to impress someone (the boss, perhaps), these influences could draw you into a risk-seeking attitude that may or may not be appropriate.

Although we are influenced by a complex mix of conscious, subconscious, and affective factors, you should try to identify key drivers. You can certainly do this for yourself when you're in a risky and important situation, and maybe others will be prepared to share too. A skilled facilitator and/or coach can help you and other group members to identify key influential factors.

As with many aspects of risk management and decision making, conversation is vital. An objective answer isn't always possible, but discussion will raise awareness and appreciation of what is going on. Some reflection on your part and a few questions to your colleagues might be all it needs to unlock a conversation that stops the group sleepwalking into a biased and suboptimal solution. It takes practice, but we'd strongly advise giving it a go.

7. I know that it's important to pay attention to weak signals—how does that fit into your approach?

The term *weak signals* is becoming part of normal business language, referring to those sources of emerging information that have the power to make or break your strategy and performance (Day & Schoemaker, 2006). It's important to build the disciplines and mindset to seek out and pay attention to weak signals.

For Risk-Intelligent Decisions, weak signals are an important part of the decision context. What is happening in the wider context that we would ignore at our peril? Some information is reliable and immediately relevant. Other information is less reliable and less immediately relevant, yet it can tell us something important about how the context may be changing, for example, the direction of travel in societal expectations, technological innovations, or the tendency of regimes to legislate or prosecute.

You may not have high confidence in the applicability of weak signals, but their value is in opening up perspectives and triggering thinking about possible future that could be relevant. Futures thinking, scenario planning, and other related techniques may be vital parts of your process to define decision information.

As always, however, the importance of paying attention to weak signals depends on how much the decision matters. It also depends on the time that it will take to implement and embed the changes associated with the decision. It's really important that you don't make decisions that will impact on the medium and long term for your organization without considering the peripheral information now that could well be mainstream by the time your change is completed.

Weak signals are also important influences in risk culture. If the culture is one in which information is ignored unless it is "proven" and/or where alternative, dissenting perspectives are eradicated before they can be heard, you are unlikely to be able to gain any advantage of honing the organizational capability of insight and peripheral vision. Your behaviors as a leader to seek out novel perspectives and non-confirmatory data will have a big effect on the wider cultural tendencies to be curious and comfortable with challenge. Building a risk culture that enables weak signals to be sought out and considered as part of the decision-making process is one key foundation stone of our approach.

8. *I work for a small company, and I have to make all strategic decisions alone. How should I modify your advice?*

Our recommendation is simple—don't do it alone! Remember the "triple strand" in Chapter 3? Your perception of risk is influenced by *conscious* rational factors, but you're also likely to be affected by *subconscious* heuristics and cognitive biases, which can have an unpredictable and unexpected effect on the decisions you make. In addition, the state of your *emotions* when you come to decide will influence your ability to think clearly. These hidden factors create blind spots that can compromise your ability to make a good decision.

You're also unlikely to have all the necessary experience, knowledge, or skills to make every strategic decision without input from others. Take a look back at the PEAKS Framework in Chapter 4; no one person has all the required elements of competence to make good decisions in every situation. No matter how mature you are in your leadership, you still have gaps that limit your decision-making ability.

Risky and important decisions matter too much for you to rely only on yourself. So even if you're the sole "official" decision maker in your small company, you can involve others in the process. Find someone else to bounce ideas off—who can act as a "critical friend" to provide another point of view as input to the decision. This might be a trusted colleague within your company who has experience or skills that you lack, or someone with a completely different attitude or background from yours who can bring a fresh perspective. You might seek input from the person who owns the strategic objectives that would be affected by a particular strategic decision, or other stakeholders, because they have a vested interest in the decision outcome and may be inclined to assist you in reaching a good decision.

If you're unable to identify a "critical friend" from within your company, you might be able to find a mentor from a professional society or business group.

Finally, if you really have to decide alone, use the Seven As Framework (from Chapter 5). Aim to become aware of your potential sources of bias (from the triple strand) and of gaps in your experience, knowledge, and skills (from the PEAKS Framework). Assess the degree to which they might affect your ability to make a good decision, and take necessary action to plug any gaps. Writing down your thoughts as you work through this process might help you decide intentionally rather than relying on your unmanaged and unreliable gut feel.

9. *My team is dysfunctional, and they don't respect my leadership. Strong characters in the team are used to getting their own way and others just roll over. They just won't accept it if I try to introduce this type of approach to decision making.*

Start somewhere and proceed by stealth. This isn't about tricking people with malicious intent but helping people become used to a situation that would be good for them! Few people welcome the "evangelist" who has just read something or been on a course that they think is important, and who then tries to implement what they've learned in one go. Don't be that person, but think what small steps you can take.

Try influencing the strong characters in the team individually, perhaps by suggesting something they can promote as their own. If that's not possible, start honing your questions to the group to prompt their thinking and planning. You could also consider how you could help empower those team members who usually "just roll over" by feeding them questions and challenges to ask.

We have mentioned the value of the neutral facilitator a number of times. A neutral person often has a much better chance of introducing a new approach than an insider does. Most people tend to be polite and give a new approach a chance if there is a credible outsider promoting the approach. It's why big consultancies do well—they have authority, experience in related organizations, and once you've decided to pay them, you want to get a return on your investment! A neutral facilitator could also be "free," perhaps someone from another part of your organization. Look for someone who can be suitably independent but is also able to act as a trusted advisor.

In summary, we'd suggest it's better to proceed slowly and gain some small and solid wins than going all out to make a big change and getting burned.

10. *Everyone in my decision-making group agrees with me, or at least they say they do. Maybe I recruited people to the team in my own image, or it might be groupthink, or possibly they really do all agree with me. What should I do?*

Here we'll start with the neutral facilitator again. Can you find someone who can challenge the group dynamics on your behalf, who is sufficiently independent and strong enough to avoid also just agreeing with you? If you can, that's one way forward, especially in the short term.

It's more important, though, to build your skills to avoid people just following the leader. It's a strange paradox that we develop leadership skills so that people will follow us, but it's counter-productive if they do so unquestioningly. One way to interrupt the routine of your decision-making group automatically agreeing with you is to adopt a "seek first to understand, then to be understood" approach (Covey, 2020). This approach emphasizes the value of understanding what others are thinking before you divulge your own thoughts and ideas. It's not always easy to do, but it's well worth trying and persevering.

What happens if you present to the group points of view that differ from your preferred way forward? How wild do these need to be for people to openly challenge you? When someone does disagree with you, encourage them, showing the team that you want people to have their own opinion and feel empowered to share it.

Encourage the team to be their own devil's advocate, thinking about and writing down the pros and cons of each decision option. If people are reluctant to speak out publicly, you could invite them to do this independently and submit it anonymously.

But if you do manage to get people to disagree with you, be careful how you react! The first time you communicate you think an idea is "stupid"—verbally or with an eye-roll or other non-verbal signal—you will destroy what you are trying to build, and people will clam up again.

So, with this challenge, others (such as a facilitator) can help you. We suggest, however, that your main focus needs to be on yourself: making sure that you can cope with challenge and discussions that may lead to a decision that wasn't your first choice.

11. *I'm self-aware enough to know that I'm not good at the people stuff. How then can I follow your advice?*

Congratulations, self-awareness is the first vital step, and it's much better than being delusionally incompetent!

Unfortunately though, "the people stuff" is central to our approach to making good decisions in risky and important situations. We fundamentally believe that people have the potential to develop if they choose to, and this includes you—you can improve your people skills! The question then becomes, who can you get to support you as you improve?

The first thing is to take stock of your natural style and preferences. If you haven't already done this, consider using psychometric tests to "look in the mirror." These can provide a valuable point of reflection on your natural preferences and predispositions. Your colleagues in HR may be able to offer suggestions of suitable models. We recommend the Hogan inventories (Hogan & Hogan, 1987), which enable you to look at your bright side (when things are going well) as well as your dark side (where you may have a tendency to over-play strengths). You might also look at specific risk-based psychometrics such as the Risk-Type Compass (Trickey, 2020).

Whether you use psychometrics or not, it's essential for you to reflect and identify specific goals in the people space. Consider using a coach to help you with this—someone who could then work with you through a practical process of development. Executive coaching is used extensively as a development tool, providing a personal, tailored experience in which you can bring your concerns and aspirations to a safe space. It's important to find someone you are comfortable to work with. Look for people who are qualified, for example, with a recognized accreditation; such coaches are bound by a code of ethics and have frequent supervision of their practice as part of their professional accreditation.

Outside of specific, professional support, we'd encourage you to have a go at following the process in this book and choosing a trusted friend or colleague to talk to, share, and work out solutions with. You already recognize that you're not good at "the people stuff," but you might be better than you think, and you can certainly improve. Practice makes perfect (or at least, it makes better!). Your leadership strengths may not be relational, but you wouldn't be where you are if you had no relevant skills, and you can build on those. If you approach the challenge with a positive mindset and a willingness to behave authentically, you might surprise yourself!

12. *My colleagues have different risk preferences from mine. How should I lead the group when we make risky and important decisions? Should I try to influence them toward my perspective?*

The first step is awareness of your natural preferences, and you can build from here.

It can be difficult when you're faced with very different preferences and perspectives, because no one's preferences are right or wrong *per se*—they're just more or less appropriate in the specific situation you are considering. We know that the attitudes we choose when faced with risky and important decisions need to be situational. This means that you may need to modify your preferred risk attitude in some situations. For example, if you're always risk averse, uncomfortable with uncertainty, and motivated to spend time and money to increase certainty, you'll be acting inappropriately in some situations.

The same goes for every other position on the risk attitude spectrum (see Figure 2.3). So, we need to define the parameters that will help us to understand whether we need to modify our starting risk attitude or not.

The key parameters here are risk thresholds. These express the risk appetite of the decision-making group in the situation, in the context of the capacity for the organization to bear the risk. Risk thresholds should be defined objectively, based on performance criteria for your organization. Be honest with yourself and your decision-making group about how much risk is too much risk—even though your preferences might be for a smaller or larger range of potential outcomes.

If you can agree on risk thresholds within the team, then making a judgment about the appropriate risk attitude follows. Listen to others in the team and work through the consequences of adopting a different risk attitude (as described in the Seven As Framework). One way of exploring the implications of risk attitudes on different decision options is to use narratives/stories to describe potential future scenarios. Storytelling enables us to access more of our brain, drawing on both facts and feelings. This can be a very useful way of helping people process their thinking and come to a consensus on the vision for the future. With a clear vision, it can be easier for people to adjust their perceptions, or at least be prepared to make a different choice that matches the appetite and capacity to take risk in the situation.

In the final analysis, if you're in charge and can make the decision on your own, you may push through your choice. Just be sure you've given it a good challenge before you do.

13. *Whenever we make a decision, everyone agrees, then no one does anything differently. How do I encourage commitment to action?*

We explained in Chapters 1 and 2 why commitment to action is a critical success factor for making good decisions, especially when those decisions are risky and important. But this needs to be understood by more than just you as the leader. Everyone needs to recognize and accept the necessity of taking action after the decision has been made, and each person must take full responsibility for their own part in implementing the agreed course of action.

The best way to achieve this is for you to have an explicit discussion about commitment to action before you come to make the decision. If you're able to draw together a specific decision-making group for a particular situation, this should form part of the briefing when you invite them to participate. Commitment to action is not an option—it's a requirement.

This may require some difficult conversations, and you may need to work with team members to find out what it would take for them to really commit, rather than merely paying lip service. Working through the Seven As Framework (Chapter 5) with your team members can be really helpful, encouraging them to express what they are thinking (Awareness), understand why they hold this position (Appreciation), determine whether it is appropriate or not (Assessment), then either move forward with confidence (Acceptance), or take steps to consciously change their approach (Assertion and Action). Keeping this conversation alive (Appraisal) reinforces the need for people to play their part in the team.

One useful way to create commitment to action where it's lacking is to clarify the link between decisions and objectives. If people care about the objectives or are invested in achieving them, then they're more likely to take action that optimizes the chances of achieving them.

Gaining commitment to action in advance is particularly important when you anticipate that decision making might involve a robust debate with individuals taking differing positions on the decision options and preferred outcomes. You need to avoid the situation in which people disengage if the decision outcome differs from their personal preferred option. Aim for "cabinet responsibility," in which the group commits to an honest and open debate during the decision-making meeting, presenting their views clearly and completely, but then each member of the group accepts the final decision and agrees to support it afterwards.

14. *I'm working with a virtual team—how can I work out what they're thinking and feeling?*

Working virtually can seem daunting. We can miss many nonverbal cues when we are not physically in the same place as others. This is compounded if people are located in places with poor connectivity or where using video is not allowed for security reasons, as you lose all visual cues. If you're in this situation, then you'll need to work hard to validate what people are thinking and feeling.

In some ways though, this may be good. Maybe we assume too much about what people are thinking and feeling when we are in the same room as them.

Sometimes virtual working is easier. For example, there tends to be more explicit permission to engage people as individuals in advance of a group session, or to get remote (and if necessary private) input.

As the technology underpinning virtual platforms continues to advance, you have really good and cheap functionality for voting, chat functions, and nonverbal reactions to get input. Creative, divergent processes can be more effective virtually as people are not as influenced by the physical presence of others, where social norms might encourage them to not share their thinking. Creating convergence of thinking as you come to a decision can also be aided by the need to share information very clearly with all parties, not just assume that everyone has the same perspective.

If you need to work more effectively in a virtual situation, we recommend Penny Pullan's book on virtual leadership (Pullan, 2016), which provides practical tips on how to excel in a virtual world.

No technology can substitute for talking to people and having ways of uncovering their thoughts rather than taking them for granted, but we'd encourage you to see virtual working as an opportunity in the context of risky and important decision making. It takes more organization to do it well, but the outcomes tend to be far less biased and therefore far more reliable.

15. *My team is multicultural—how should I take account of different cultural norms?*

Our earlier research explored factors that influence the way groups operate in risky situations (Murray-Webster & Hillson, 2008), and we discovered that these factors could be divided into two categories. The primary category of strongest influences included individuals with high levels of power and propinquity, the decision context, the organizational culture, and group dynamics. We also identified a secondary category of influences which were less significant, including low-power individuals, societal norms, and national cultural characteristics. These secondary factors were less likely to drive group behavior in risky situations. In fact, our research revealed that national culture was the weakest influence out of the eight factors we examined.

This doesn't mean that national culture is irrelevant when you're working with a multicultural team to make risky and important decisions. But it does suggest that there are many other factors that are more influential, and you can use these to counter the effect of national culture where necessary.

For example, you're naturally in a higher power position as leader, and you can use this to persuade others toward accepting a particular decision outcome. You can also appeal to the organizational culture (where this is helpful), which team members should perceive as more influential than their own national cultural preferences. In addition, you can use the behavioral literacy approaches outlined in Chapter 5 to moderate the group dynamics in your decision-making group, encouraging consensus and commitment to action. You can also work on developing a mature risk culture (as discussed in Chapter 6), which will have a bigger effect on the decision-making approach than the cultural preferences of individuals.

Despite all this, it is nevertheless vital for you as leader to be aware of the sensitivities and values associated with the national cultures of your team members. Your communication style will be particularly important here, being respectful of the cultural norms of others, remaining inclusive, while clearly providing boundaries and guidelines to keep the group on track together. You must also be aware of different perspectives on authority which may make some team members reluctant to speak up with a different opinion or unwilling to challenge you as leader.

You may wish to undertake some training in cultural intelligence, if you regularly work with multicultural teams. This could usefully be extended to the whole decision-making group, to ensure that everyone knows how to handle cultural differences. Another option is to use a culturally sensitive facilitator to support your decision-making meetings.

7.1 Key Points

This chapter has provided the following key insights:

- When it comes to implementing theory, there are often difficulties in practice.
- You might have felt that some aspects of the generic approach described in previous chapters could be hard to apply in your specific situation. Fortunately, there are answers to the most commonly asked questions if you want to address performance in this area.
- Making risky and important decisions is a hard task and a significant challenge. There's no silver bullet that ensures a good decision every time—you have to work at it. But these decisions are vital, by definition, so it's worth putting in the time and effort to make the best possible decision in the situation you face.

7.2 Looking Forward

We have one more chapter to go. In Chapter 8 we sum up the key points from the book and provide a call to action. Hopefully you'll be motivated to change something in the way you lead decision making in risky and important situations.

References

Covey, S. R. (2020). *The 7 Habits of Highly Effective People*, 30th anniversary edition. New York: Simon and Schuster.

Day, G. S., and Schoemaker, P. J. H. (2006). *Peripheral Vision: Detecting the Weak Signals That Will Make or Break Your Company.* Boston, MA: Harvard Business School Press.

Hauser, J. R., and Clausing, D. P. (1988). The house of quality. *Harvard Business Review,* May/June.

Hogan, J., and Hogan, R. (1987). Hogan psychometric tools. https://www.hogan assessments.com

Murray-Webster, R., and Hillson, D. A. (2008). *Managing Group Risk Attitude.* Aldershot, UK: Gower Publishing.

Pullan, P. (2016). *Virtual Leadership: Practical Strategies for Getting the Most of Our Virtual Work and Virtual Teams.* London, UK: Kogan Page.

Trickey, G. (2020). The risk-type compass. https://www.psychological-consul tancy.com/products/risk-type-compass/

Willem de Kooning, quoted in Jack Cowart, "De Kooning today." *Art International* (Summer 1979), 16.

Chapter 8

You Can Do It!

We started this book with an assertion, an observation, and an objective:

- *Our assertion:* As a leader, a large part of your role is to make decisions.
- *Our observation:* Decisiveness—the ability to make decisions quickly and effectively—is a highly valued trait of leaders in many cultures.
- *Our objective:* To provide you with a practical guide to making those "big" decisions that need to be taken from time to time (we call these *risky and important decisions*).

To recap the starting premise in Chapter 1, we define decisions as risky and important when:

- The impact on strategic or long-term operational objectives is significant.
- The context is complex, unstable, or changing.
- There is a significant amount of risk associated with different options, and comparing options and their impact on objectives is not straightforward.
- There is no guarantee of commitment from the people who you need to support and implement the chosen outcome.

We want you to close this book knowing what you can do to hone your skills, navigate your complex world, and lead your team to make these kinds of decisions more effectively, more of the time. Before we finish, however, there are four remaining challenges to address.

8.1 Four Key Challenges

We know you can improve the way that risky and important decisions are taken, and we want you to be confident that you can make a positive difference. To support you in meeting these goals, we've covered a number of areas spanning decision-making processes and behaviors so that you can confidently answer the questions we raised in Chapter 1:

- How much risk is too much risk for my organization?
- How is my personal view influencing my judgment?
- How can I balance reason and intuition?
- How can I inspire and embed the behaviors needed to build an effective culture?

8.1.1 How Much Risk Is Too Much Risk for My Organization?

In Chapter 2 we explored the process for making a Risk-Intelligent Decision. There are many variables involved in this process, all aimed at understanding how much risk would be too much risk and then adjusting options and choices to match two things: (1) the expression of risk appetite, and (2) the capacity to bear risk.

Chapter 2 concluded that before making a decision, you need to understand both the *decision information* (objectives, context, and options), and the *decision makers* (especially their individual risk preferences, shared risk culture, and commitment to action). It's vital to know the level of risk associated with each decision option. This is driven by risk perception, which may not be reliable. You also need to know how much risk is tolerable. This requires you to understand your risk appetite and express it in measurable risk thresholds, then choose a decision option that lies within the thresholds. If no decision option falls within your initial risk thresholds, it's possible, with the help of the Seven As Framework, to choose a different risk attitude and modify thresholds accordingly.

The process focus in Chapter 2 enables you to link all the parts of our advice together, to see what you have in place and what is missing and to see how the parts influence the whole.

8.1.2 How Is My Personal View Influencing My Judgment?

Hopefully you are convinced by now, even if you weren't so sure at the start of the book, that we all "get in the way" of good decisions from time to time. Your judgments can be skewed by all sorts of conscious and subconscious factors. This is bad enough if you're making decisions alone, but the problem is compounded when a decision-making group is involved.

When you're approaching a risky and important decision, you might feel that you understand how *important* it is, but you can't know for sure how *risky* it is. Your judgment is based on your perception of the level of risk. But risk perception is influenced by many factors, and it may not be a reliable indicator of true riskiness.

The "triple strand" described in Chapter 3 groups influences on risk perception into three categories: *conscious* (rational assessments), *subconscious* (heuristics and cognitive biases), and *affective* (gut-level feelings and emotions). You need to understand these before you can take account of them, for yourself and for your decision-making group.

You can't completely "unpick" the combined effect, but you can identify the key drivers that are influencing your judgment so you can check out whether this is appropriate or not.

8.1.3 How Can I Balance Reason and Intuition?

Reason and intuition are both important. We don't intend to suggest we can reduce decision making in risky and important situations to a set of rules to be followed. But leaving everything to intuition is suboptimal, even if we label this intuition as experience (!) to make it seem more rational.

One key step in balancing reason and intuition is to really understand the decision-making group. This involves understanding their competencies as individuals (Personal characteristics, Experience, Attitudes, Knowledge, and Skills, or PEAKS) and their collective capabilities and tendencies, including factors that make them more likely to be drawn into systemically biased behaviors. The other key step is to then really engage members of the group to understand different viewpoints, perspectives, and solutions before coming to a decision.

This is the most difficult part of decision making for many leaders, particularly if you are working in a culture in which everyone looks to you to be a single decisive voice, or you feel that's what you should be providing. As leader, you may need to work with individuals in your team who have limited decision-making competence. Some aspects of group behavior may also need your attention, as we outlined in Chapter 4. To address this, in Chapter 5 we suggested the structured Seven As Framework, starting with Awareness, Appreciation, and Assessment. This may lead to Acceptance of the status quo, or Assertion and Action may be needed in order to produce change. Either way, the framework includes Appraisal, to check whether anything significant has changed. In recommending the Seven As Framework, we offer a logical series of steps to check out whether change is needed, while at the same time recognizing that the work to complete each of the steps requires emotional maturity and behavioral literacy.

8.1.4 How Can I Inspire and Embed the Behaviors Needed to Build an Effective Culture?

An appropriate risk culture is one that enables the exposure of information that is complete enough to support the weight of the decision and one that can understand and modify hidden influences on perception and choice under uncertainty. You can influence the prevailing culture through encouraging different behavior, and this requires you to understand which behaviors and characteristics you can allow to flourish and which you need to change.

In Chapter 6 we outlined four aspects of behavior that are essential for shaping a mature risk culture: how you communicate, how you enable information sharing, how you support people, and how you recognize and reward risk taking. As a leader and role model in your organization, you have a direct impact on the ability of your team to understand risk, to speak about it with confidence, and to appreciate how their perceptions and those of others might be biased.

Inspiring others to improve their understanding and practice in risky and important decisions is down to you.

8.2 You Really Can Do It!

We started Chapter 1 by suggesting that you could "do better," improving the way that you take decisions and lead others in decision making. Throughout this book, we've highlighted the factors that influence the quality of a risky and important decision, and we've provided suggestions and tips on how you can improve and drive improvement.

The approach we've described in this book provides a blend of *process* and *people,* because both are vital components when making a good decision. You'll inevitably need to pay attention to both process and people aspects if you're going to improve your decision making. It's essential for you to get the right balance between reason, rules, and data on the one hand, and intuition, behaviors, and competence on the other, as illustrated in Figure 8.1.

We know our approach will have raised many questions for you. In Chapter 7 we've dealt with 15 of the questions that we're most commonly asked, providing our advice on how to tackle them. We hope you will have taken some inspiration and encouragement from knowing that others have expressed similar concerns and that helpful answers are available.

Figure 8.1   Effective Decision Making Balances Process and People Aspects

Luck will always play a part when you're making risky and important decisions. You can't control luck, but you can influence the quality of the decision-making process you follow. The most important thing is to do something! Having invested your time and effort in reading this far, you need to act on what you've learned if you don't want it to be wasted. We advise you to start small. Try implementing some things that you think will make a difference, then reflect on how things have changed, and keep building.

This book is not about every decision you make, just the ones that are risky and important. It's also not about trying to get the *right* answer, because there isn't one. If you can accept the complexity of risky and important decision making and see ways to lead through that complexity with foresight and insight, we believe that you will see great results.

We wish you well.

Appendix A

Recommended Further Reading

The ideas (and shortcomings) in this book are our own, but we've drawn on the work of others in developing our approach. Each chapter ends with a specific set of relevant references, but this appendix offers additional key sources that more broadly complement our thinking. For each chapter of our book, we present here one recommended reference that deserves your attention if you want to delve deeper into the topic.

Leach, P. (2014). *Why Can't You Just Give Me the Number? An Executive's Guide to Using Probabilistic Thinking to Manage Risk and to Make Better Decisions*, 2nd edition. Sugar Land, TX: Probabilistic Publishing.

> Written for people who need to understand how to make better risk-based decisions, this is a really practical read that covers the challenges we all face when decision makers just want to know, "When can I have it, and how much will it cost?" We know that the worst thing we can do is to anchor them to a single-point estimate (especially an optimistic one!) with no real understanding of confidence levels. A good companion to the Risk-Intelligent Decision model in Chapter 2.

Ariely, D. (2008). *Predictably Irrational: The Hidden Forces That Shape Our Decisions*. New York: Harper Collins.

One of the first "easy-read" books that challenged rational-choice theories and gave compelling examples of how real decisions fall foul of heuristics and cognitive biases. A very readable deeper dive into some of the Chapter 3 content.

Sustein, C. R., and Hastie, R. (2015). *Wiser: Getting Beyond Groupthink to Make Groups Smarter*. Brighton, MA: Harvard Business Review Press.

A solidly researched yet entertaining read that makes the case for decision-making groups being better than individuals every time. The authors share practical ways that groups can avoid their greatest pitfall—caring too much about social cohesion and therefore falling foul to groupthink. A good companion to Chapter 4.

Stavros, J., and Torres, C. (2018). *Conversations Worth Having: Using Appreciative Inquiry to Fuel Productive and Meaningful Engagement*. Oakland, CA: Berrett-Koehler Publishers.

A key aspect of getting the Seven As Framework to work as described in Chapter 5 is an appreciation of others' points of view, and getting to this requires conversation. This is a really practical book about questions to ask and approaches to take to enable conversations that are productive.

Kegan, R., and Lahey, L. L. (2002). *How the Way We Talk Can Change the Way We Work: Seven Languages for Transformation*. San Francisco, CA: Jossey-Bass.

The title is a classic "does what it says on the cover." The book provides inspiration and instruction to help us understand how we talk and how that impacts the way we work and (crucially) the impact we have on others when we are trying to lead change. An excellent companion for all leaders of change, including those trying to change risk culture, as described in Chapter 6.

Duke, A. (2020). *How to Decide: Simple Tools for Making Better Choices.* New York: Penguin Publishing Group.

A practical book you can use to train yourself to become more aware of your biases and more confident when making big decisions. As we suggest multiple times in Chapter 7, improving your leadership of risky and important decision making starts with you, and this book will be a helpful companion.

Appendix B

Further Reading from the Authors

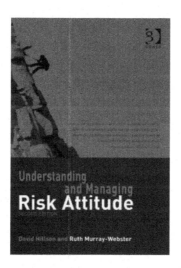

UNDERSTANDING AND MANAGING
RISK ATTITUDE, 2nd edition

David Hillson and Ruth Murray-Webster (Routledge, 2007)

Risk attitude is one of the key variables in making risky and important decisions, and it needs to be both understood and managed. But although it's often discussed, risk attitude is not always well understood.

Risk attitude depends on how we perceive risk, and risk perception in turn is affected by multiple influences. In *Understanding and Managing Risk Attitude*, we define and explore the core idea of the "triple strand of influences" on perception and risk attitude. We also explain that risk attitude is not good or bad, per se, but it is highly situational. Chapter 3 of *Making Risky and Important Decisions: A Leader's Guide* provides a summary of this work on understanding risk attitude, presented in relation to making risky and important decisions. In the original book, there is more information to help you consider your own attitude in different situations. Beyond the simplistic thinking that, "I am always risk tolerant," or, "You are always risk averse," risk attitude is a choice. Many times we adopt an attitude to risk unquestioningly, through habit and/or deeply rooted psychological preferences. This may be sensible on some occasions, particularly where the situation is routine and familiar to us. But it is not sensible to be unquestioning all the time, particularly when the situation is non-routine and the stakes are high. So, thinking of risk attitude as a choice is important.

How can risk attitude be managed? In the first edition of *Understanding and Managing Risk Attitude* (2005), we brought together leading thinking on emotional literacy with leading thinking on risk for the first time. If risk attitude is fundamentally a choice, yet habits, heuristics, cognitive biases, and emotions have such a biasing effect, what skills do people need to be able to choose?

Drawing from the work of risk psychology and the study of social interactions and applying this to choices made under uncertainty, we provide an in-depth explanation of how to intentionally modify attitude. This work is a key contributor to Chapter 5 of *Making Risky and Important Decisions: A Leader's Guide*, with the Seven As Framework. In the original book, we explore the underpinning rationale for the importance of awareness of self and appreciation of points of view different from your own. Sometimes it's necessary to choose a risk attitude which differs from your starting point. This requires intentionality and can involve assertiveness and conflict resolution—all topics covered in detail in the book. If you want a deeper dive into risk attitude from an individual point of view, *Understanding and Managing Risk Attitude* will meet that need.

ISBN: 978-0-566-08798-1
https://www.routledge.com/9780566087981

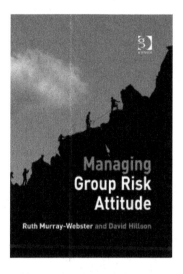

MANAGING GROUP RISK ATTITUDE
Ruth Murray-Webster and David Hillson (Routledge, 2008)

Understanding and Managing Risk Attitude explored risk attitude as a choice from an individual point of view, and *Managing Group Risk Attitude* builds on those insights to focus specifically on the influences on perception and choice experienced by both groups as a whole and individuals working in decision-making groups. Based on our own experience and ground-breaking research, this book explores how groups of people make decisions that they perceive as risky and important. A unique framework is developed and applied, providing a practical model using applied emotional literacy to manage group risk attitude. This in turn allows boards, senior management teams, and other groups to improve their decision making in the face of uncertainty, ensuring that they are able to take the right risks safely.

The book starts by exploring what was already known about influences on group behavior, ranging from biasing effects such as groupthink through to the effects of organizational and national cultural differences. We then undertook detailed phenomenological research based on real decisions in order to identify the most influential factors on the final decisions taken. We exposed important underlying patterns about the critical influences on people working in decision-making groups, and these findings are summarized in Chapter 4 of *Making Risky and Important Decisions: A Leader's Guide.*

As with *Understanding and Managing Risk Attitude,* our intention in this book is not merely to diagnose the influences on groups making risky and important decisions. We are also committed to providing practical advice on how to manage the various factors that affect group decision making. This leads to the original Six As Framework, which we have further developed in Chapter 5 of *Making Risky and Important Decisions: A Leader's Guide* into the Seven As Framework.

Managing Group Risk Attitude is the place to go if you are interested in understanding risk attitude from a group point of view, drawing on multiple examples of real decisions in organizations, and learning from things that can go wrong in practice.

ISBN: 978-0-566-08787-5
https://www.routledge.com/9780566087875

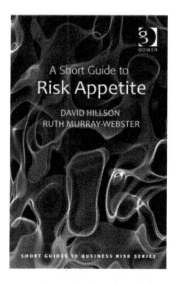

A SHORT GUIDE TO RISK APPETITE
David Hillson and Ruth Murray-Webster (Routledge, 2012)

Risk appetite is a different concept from *risk attitude*, yet the two are often confused. Along with other important risk concepts such as risk capacity, risk thresholds, and risk exposure, *A Short Guide to Risk Appetite* was written to help practitioners understand how concepts differed and, importantly, how they relate to the task of decision making. This book cuts through the confusion to produce clear definitions and simple guidelines, answering the all-important question: "How much risk should we take?" It is another important prequel to *Making Risky and Important Decisions: A Leader's Guide* in that it introduces the idea of the Risk-Intelligent Decision and contrasts this to decisions that are, in some way or other, made with eyes closed/risk blind or at least some degree of risk myopia.

This book was published at a time when the concept of risk appetite was becoming increasingly important to corporate governance. In many countries, but particularly in the UK, directors of listed companies were explicitly tasked with defining their appetite for risk in creating value for shareholders. Senior leaders in organizations were exploring how best to understand and define risk appetite, particularly to express risk appetite for non-financial objectives that impact on reputation alongside risk appetite for financial performance.

It was through our work on this book and a wide range of consulting assignments thereafter that many senior leaders began to appreciate that expressing risk appetite is a vital aspect of managing performance. Directors who were expecting a conversation about risk realized that risk appetite was primarily about defining strategy and performance. Only with appetite defined and expressed as measurable thresholds can risk be effectively managed, through the choice of an appropriate risk attitude.

In addition to providing a workable process for understanding and expressing risk appetite, this book provides clear explanations of key risk-related terms and the interactions between them. Armed with these definitions, you'll have all you need to ensure that your exposure to risk remains within your risk appetite and your risk capacity.

ISBN: 978-1-4094-4094-9
https://www.routledge.com/9781409440949

EXPLOITING FUTURE UNCERTAINTY
David Hillson (Routledge, 2010)

As a leader charged with making risky and important decisions, you have to consider lots of different aspects at the same time. It's tempting to remain above the detail, to take a helicopter approach or bird's-eye view, especially where specialist disciplines are involved. When it comes to risk, you need a certain level of understanding, but you don't have to be a risk expert, and you'll probably be able to leave the specifics to someone else.

Although this is generally the case, there will be times when you need a quick refresher on a particular risk topic, perhaps to enable you to have a sensible discussion with an expert, to properly assess the risk associated with a decision option, or to understand some specific aspects of a decision context. Where do you go at times like these?

Exploiting Future Uncertainty is designed for the busy executive or practitioner who needs reliable information on a particular risk topic but who doesn't have time to read a detailed textbook or watch a lengthy training video. This practical guide contains over 60 focused briefings, each addressing a key part of the risk challenge. Each topic covers just two or three pages, allowing you to find what you need quickly and gain a clear understanding of the subject.

The topics in this book are arranged under five themes, covering:

- Basic risk concepts
- Risk management in practice
- People aspects
- Linking better business to risk taking
- Managing risk in the wider world

Whether you read a complete section or dip into a particular topic, you'll find clear practical advice with specific how-to tips and guidance that you can implement immediately. As a busy leader making risky and important decisions, this book will prove to be an indispensable companion when you need good risk information quickly.

ISBN: 978-1-4094-2341-6
https://www.routledge.com/9781409423416

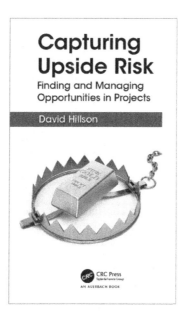

CAPTURING UPSIDE RISK
David Hillson (Auerbach Publications, 2019)

Before you can make a risky and important decision, you need to be clear about what you mean by "risk." To many people, risk is a potentially bad thing to be avoided or minimized. With this view, the aim of a risky and important decision is to give yourself the best chance of achieving your decision objectives *despite* the risks associated with the decision context and decision options.

However, current thinking about risk is very different. Starting with the concept that risk is "uncertainty that matters," it quickly becomes clear that some uncertainties would matter because they could be bad news if they were to happen, but there are other uncertainties which matter because they could be positive and helpful if they occurred. In this approach, "risk" includes two equally important sides: negative downside risks (also known as threats), and positive upside risks (called opportunities). Following on from this, risk management is about more than preventing harm and protecting value. It also means finding ways to enhance benefits and create value. We need to minimize threats and maximize opportunities *at the same time* if we are to optimize our chances of achieving our objectives.

In the context of making risky and important decisions, you need to consider both threat and opportunity as you decide how much risk to take. Where there is significant upside, this might mean adopting a more risk-seeking attitude in order to improve your chance of capturing opportunities and turning them into value.

Perhaps like many others, you're familiar with the idea that risk is double-sided, including both threat and opportunity. But maybe you're unsure about how to put this theory into practice. *Capturing Upside Risk* provides clear advice on how to make this work in real life. The book begins by answering the question, "What are opportunities?," starting from first principles to explain the nature of risk. The body of this unique book then explains in detail how to both create and protect value by managing opportunities and threats together through an integrated risk process. Proven tools and techniques are described, offering guidance on how you can find and capture opportunities. While the focus of this book is on identifying, assessing, and managing opportunities in projects, the principles and concepts are more widely applicable, including at business and strategic levels.

The insights into the nature of risk contained in *Capturing Upside Risk* will help you make better decisions, especially when they are risky and important. Neglecting upside risk means you'll be making decisions with one arm tied behind your back and a patch over one eye, denying yourself the additional value and benefits that can arise from exploiting opportunities fully.

ISBN: 978-0-8153-8251-5
https://www.routledge.com/9780815382515

MANAGING RISK IN PROJECTS
David Hillson (Routledge, 2011)

Don't let the title put you off! *Managing Risk in Projects* is aimed squarely at project managers and other project professionals who need to understand and manage risk in the project arena. But this short book is packed with valuable information that's directly relevant to anyone facing uncertainty at any level of business, not just relating to projects. A quick run through the chapter headings is enough to see how this book can be helpful to you as a leader. As a minimum, it will help you lead your project teams more effectively, asking the right questions, providing appropriate encouragement and direction, and giving them the support they need to deliver successful projects for your organization and your stakeholders. But this little book has much more to offer you that's directly relevant to your own challenges as a leader:

- **Uncertainty and risk.** Starting from first principles, we discover why all risks are uncertain, but not all uncertainties are risks. This insight provides a firm foundation for understanding why risk matters and why managing risk might be the most important thing we can do.
- **Risk and projects.** In line with the book's title, we explain why all projects are risky and how the "zero-risk project" is a myth.

- **Managing risk in practice.** Process is necessary but not sufficient, and we provide a generic set of questions as a structuring framework to define what steps are required when we're managing risk.
- **Risk and people.** Risk is managed by people, not processes, and we're complex beings affected by multiple influences, both seen and unseen. We introduce risk attitude as a key driver of behavior, including decision making.
- **Integrating risk management with wider project management.** Risk management isn't a standalone discipline, so we explore how all other project management processes need to be informed by an understanding of risk.
- **The bigger picture.** Risk affects much more than projects, and here we raise our sights to include the wider strategic horizon. How should our understanding of risk exposure affect the way we lead the organization as a whole?
- **Making risk management work.** We end by considering how to make management of risk sustainable, with practical guidance on creating and maintaining energy throughout the organization to ensure that adequate attention is given to risk.

If you're leading a project-based business or your organization delivers value to stakeholders through projects and programs, you need to know how to manage risk in projects. But this book offers much more, with concise coverage of the wider risk landscape that will help you address the risk challenges you face in all areas of your business, including risky and important decision making.

ISBN: 978-0-566-08867-4
https://www.routledge.com/9780566088674

A SHORT GUIDE TO FACILITATING RISK MANAGEMENT
Penny Pullan and Ruth Murray-Webster (Routledge, 2011)

We know that it is a key competency of organizations to take risks to create value and to manage risk to prevent value destruction or erosion over time. We also know that doing this well is not a simple task. Many publications exist that focus on a risk process, including international standards (ISO31000: 2018), industry guides, and many books. Despite all of this—and our own published work aimed at clearly explaining the nature of uncertainties that matter, both upside opportunities and downside threats, and dealing with the important yet often misunderstood concepts of risk appetite and risk attitude—there is more to do in practice.

The difficulties of putting solid risk theory into practice are largely associated with the nature of risk—that it is a future construct that only *might* occur, and therefore busy leaders could be forgiven for focusing their time on things actually happening now. Of course, managing risk well reduces surprises and problems, but an act of faith is required to build enough organizational ability to see the fruits of this labor. Part of the work is about building an appropriate risk culture, and we address your leadership role in building an appropriate risk culture in Chapter 6 of *Making Risky and Important Decisions: A Leader's Guide.* In *A Short Guide to Facilitating Risk Management,* Ruth, writing with Penny Pullan, goes back to basics to help those people tasked with making the risk process work in practice.

Facilitation of the risk process is key. There are many biasing influences on each step of a risk process, from expressing appetite in a measurable way, identifying risks, determining the priority of risks, and deciding if and how to respond to risks. Without neutral facilitation and challenge, it is extremely difficult for leaders to get appropriate outcomes from the investment they put into risk discussions. Risk workshops have been popular for many years. Without great facilitation they can be deeply dysfunctional. Many parts of the risk process benefit from independent input prior to sharing with groups. Working with individuals or groups can happen virtually or in person. *A Short Guide to Facilitating Risk Management* provides clear, simple advice on what to do and how to avoid the many pitfalls that exist. People who have tried to get risk working in their organizations share their stories, and alternative approaches to achieving the same end are highlighted.

If risk management is important, and we believe it is, this book provides invaluable advice to practitioners who need to engage others to identify, own, and manage risk.

ISBN: 978-1-4094-0730-0
https://www.routledge.com/9781409407300

Glossary

A-B-C Model: A generic model of culture, reflecting interrelationships among Attitudes, Behavior, and Culture.

Competence: The ability to do a specific task or role effectively, measured in terms of behavior and performance that can be observed in practice.

Decision objectives: The desired outcomes to be achieved as a result of making this decision.

PEAKS Framework: A generic competence framework that defines five elements of competence:

- Personal characteristics (natural preferences and traits that form the basis of a person's style and natural reactions to situations).
- Experience (acquired in formal roles and other life contexts, measured by relevant achievements, relative to the needs of a specific organizational requirement).
- Attitudes (chosen responses to situations).
- Knowledge (familiarity with widely held principles about a particular subject and the way those principles should be applied to best effect).
- Skills (application of other elements of competence in pursuit of defined objectives).

Risk: Uncertainty that matters.

Risk action: Action taken to respond to risk exposure, ideally as part of a structured risk process.

Risk appetite: Tendency of an individual or group to take risk in a given situation.

Risk attitude: Chosen response of an individual or group to a given risky situation, influenced by risk perception.

Risk averse: A risk attitude that is uncomfortable with uncertainty, with a desire to avoid or reduce threats and exploit opportunities to remove uncertainty.

Risk-Blind Decision: A decision taken with no conscious assessment of the riskiness of the decision or the appropriateness of the result.

Risk capacity: Ability of an entity to bear risk, quantified against objectives.

Risk culture: The values, beliefs, knowledge, and understanding about risk shared by a group of people with a common purpose.

Risk exposure: A measure of the overall effect of identified risks on objectives. Risk exposure may be expressed quantitatively or qualitatively.

Risk-Informed Decision: A decision that considers risk explicitly and chooses an option that stays within the limits of defined risk thresholds.

Risk-Intelligent Decision: A decision that reflects the decision objectives, context, options, and commitment to action; individual risk preferences and shared risk culture; perception of the degree of risk exposure associated with each decision option; explicit consideration of risk appetite, expressed in risk thresholds; and a chosen risk attitude that maximizes the chances of achieving decision objectives.

Risk perception: View of risky situation by individual or group, influenced by "triple strand" (conscious, subconscious, and affective) factors.

Risk preference: Those aspects of an individual's personality and motivation that influence their risk propensity.

Risk propensity: Tendency of an individual to take risks in general, informed by inherent risk preferences.

Risk seeking: A risk attitude that is comfortable with uncertainty, with no desire to avoid or reduce threats or to exploit opportunities to remove uncertainty.

Risk thresholds: Quantified measures that represent upper and lower limits of acceptable uncertainty against each objective.

Risk tolerant: A risk attitude that is tolerant of uncertainty, with no strong desire to respond to threats or opportunities in any way.

Risky and important decision: A decision for which the impact on strategic or long-term operational objectives is significant; the context is complex, unstable, or changing; there is a significant amount of risk associated with different options; comparing options and their impact on objectives is not straightforward; there is no guarantee of commitment from the people who are required to support and implement the chosen outcome.

Seven As Framework: An applied behavioral literacy model allowing an individual to modify the behaviors of themself and others in an intentional and deliberate way in order to optimize the chances of achieving a desired outcome. The framework has seven stages: Awareness, Appreciation, Assessment, Acceptance, Assertion, Action, Appraisal.

Triple strand: Influences on risk perception, arranged into three categories:

- *Conscious* factors (situational characteristics of a particular risky and important decision that can be observed, counted, and measured and that can be described and assessed in a rational way despite the presence of uncertainty).
- *Subconscious* factors (heuristics and cognitive biases that lie below the level of conscious or rational awareness).
- *Affective* factors (gut-level visceral feelings and emotions that arise automatically or instinctively in a situation).

Index

Printed in the United States
by Baker & Taylor Publisher Services